The Yellow Wind

David Grossman

The Yellow Wind

Translated from the Hebrew

by Haim Watzman

Farrar, Straus and Giroux

New York

Copyright © 1988 by David Grossman and Koteret Rashit
Translation copyright © 1988 by Haim Watzman
All rights reserved
Printed in the United States of America
Published simultaneously in Canada by
Collins Publishers, Toronto
First edition, 1988
Library of Congress Cataloging-in-Publication Data
Grossman, David.
    The yellow wind.
    Translation of: ha-Zeman ha-tsahov.
    1. West Bank—Description and travel. 2. Jewish-Arab
relations—1973–   . 3. Grossman, David—Journeys—
West Bank. I. Title.
DS110.W47G7613   1988   956.95'3   87-37527

Portions of this book first appeared in
The New Yorker in a slightly different form.
Grateful acknowledgment is made to Harcourt Brace
Jovanovich, Inc., and the Estate of the late Sonia
Brownell Orwell and Secker and Warburg Limited
for permission to reprint sections of "Shooting an
Elephant" from Shooting an Elephant and Other
Essays by George Orwell, copyright 1950 by Sonia
Brownell Orwell; renewed 1978 by Sonia Pitt-Rivers

Contents

The Yellow Wind

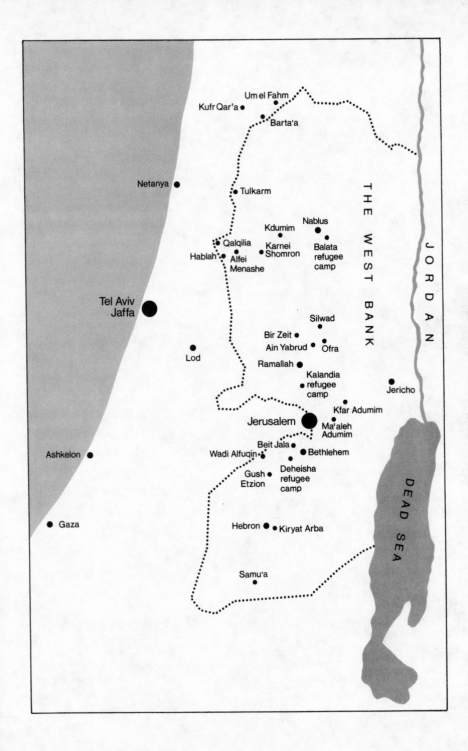

1

A Man Is Like

a Stalk of Wheat

On a day of turbid rain, at the end of March, I turn
off the main road leading from my house in Jerusalem
to Hebron, and enter the Deheisha refugee camp. Twelve
thousand Palestinians live here in one of the highest
population densities in the world; the houses are piled
together, and the house of every extended family branches
out in ugly cement growths, rooms and niches, rusty
iron beams spread throughout as sinews, jutting like
disconnected fingers.

In Deheisha, drinking water comes from wells. The
only running water is the rainwater and sewage flowing
down the paths between the houses. I soon give up picking my way between the puddles; there is something
ridiculous—almost unfair—about preserving such refinement here, in the face of a few drops of filth.

Beside each house—a yard. They are small, fenced in
with corrugated aluminum, and very clean. A large *jara*
filled with springwater and covered with cloth stands in
each yard. But every person here will tell you without
hesitation that the water from the spring of his home

village was sweeter. "In Ain Azrab"—she sighs (her name is Hadija, and she is very old)—"our water was so clear and healthy that a dying man once immersed himself, drank a few mouthfuls, and washed—and was healed on the spot." She cocks her head, drills me with an examining gaze, and mocks: "So, what do you think of that?"

I discover—with some bafflement, I admit—that she reminds me of my grandmother and her stories about Poland, from which she was expelled. About the river, about the fruit there. Time has marked both their faces with the same lines, of wisdom and irony, of great skepticism toward all people, both relatives and strangers.

"We had a field there. A vineyard. Now see what a flowering garden we have here," and she waves her brown, wrinkled hand over the tiny yard.

"But we made a garden," murmurs her daughter-in-law, a woman of wild, gypsy, unquiet beauty. "We made a garden in tin cans." She nods toward the top of the cinder-block fence, where several pickle cans bring forth red geraniums, in odd abundance, as if drawing their life from some far source of fruitfulness, of creation.

A strange life. Double and split. Everyone I spoke to in the camp is trained—almost from birth—to live this double life: they sit here, very much here, because deprivation imposes sobriety with cruel force, but they are also there. That is—among us. In the villages, in the cities. I ask a five-year-old boy where he is from, and he immediately answers, "Jaffa," which is today part of Tel Aviv. "Have you ever seen Jaffa?" "No, but my grandfather saw it." His father, apparently, was born here, but his grandfather came from Jaffa. "And is it beautiful, Jaffa?" "Yes. It has orchards and vineyards and the sea."

And farther down, where the path slopes, I meet a young girl sitting on a cement wall, reading an illustrated magazine. Where are you from? She is from Lod, not far from Ben-Gurion International Airport, forty years ago an Arab town. She is sixteen. She tells me, giggling, of the beauty of Lod. Of its houses, which were big as palaces. "And in every room a hand-painted carpet. And the land was wonderful, and the sky was always blue."

I remembered the wistful lines of Yehuda Halevy, "The taste of your sand—more pleasant to my mouth than honey," and Bialik, who sang to the land which "the spring eternally adorns," how wonderfully separation beautifies the beloved, and how strange it is, in the barrenness of the gray cement of Deheisha, to hear sentences so full of lyric beauty, words spoken in a language more exalted than the everyday, poetic but of established routine, like a prayer or an oath: "And the tomatoes there were red and big, and everything came to us from the earth, and the earth gave us and gave us more."

"Have you visited there, Lod?" "Of course not." "Aren't you curious to see it now?" "Only when we return."

This is how the others answer me also. The Palestinians, as is well known, are making use of the ancient Jewish strategy of exile and have removed themselves from history. They close their eyes against harsh reality, and stubbornly clamping down their eyelids, they fabricate their Promised Land. "Next year in Jerusalem," said the Jews in Latvia and in Cracow and in San'a, and the meaning was that they were not willing to compromise. Because they had no hope for any real change. He who has nothing to lose can demand everything; and until his Jerusalem becomes real, he will do nothing to bring it closer. And here also, again and again, that absolute demand: everything. Nablus and Hebron and Jaffa and Jerusalem. And in the meantime—nothing. In the meantime, abandoned physically and spiritually. In the meantime, a dream and a void.

It's all bolitics, the Palestinians say. Even those who can pronounce the "p" in "politics" will say "bolitics," as a sign of defiance, in which there is a sort of self-mocking; "bolitics," which means that whole game being played over our heads, kept out of our hands, crushing us for decades under all the occupations, sucking out of us life and the power to act, turning us into dust, it's all bolitics, the Turks and the British, and the son-of-a-whore Hussein who killed and slaughtered us without mercy, and now all of a sudden he makes himself out to be the protector of the Palestinians, and these Israelis, who are willing to bring down a government because of two terrorists they killed in a bus, and with the considered cruelty of an impeccably meticulous jurist they change our laws, one thousand two hundred new laws they issued, and deprive us of our land and of our tradition and of our honor, and construct for us here some kind of great enlightened prison, when all they really want is for us to escape from it, and then they won't let us return to it ever—and in their proud cunning, which we are completely unable to understand, they bind their strings to us, and we dance for them like marionettes.

"It's all bolitics," laughs the ironic woman, who reminds me slightly of my grandmother, and slightly of the cunning, old, loud Italian from *Catch-22*, the one who explains to proud American Nately why America will lose the war in the end, and poor Italy will not win, but survive. "The strongest weapon the Arabs in the occupied territories can deploy against us," a wise man once said, "is not to change." And it is true—when you walk through the Deheisha camp you feel as if that conception has internalized itself unconsciously here, seeped its way into the hearts of the people and become power, defiance: we will not change, we will not try to improve our lives. We will remain before you like a curse cast in cement.

She suddenly remembers: "There, in the village, in Ain Azrab, we baked bread over a straw fire. Not here. Because here we don't have livestock, and none of their leavings." She falls silent and hugs herself. Her forehead wrinkles repeatedly in a spasm of wonder. The brown, wrinkled fingers go, unconsciously, through the motions of kneading.

Everything happens elsewhere. Not now. In another place. In a splendid past or a longed-for future. The thing most present here is absence. Somehow one senses that people here have turned themselves voluntarily into doubles of the real people who once were, in another place. Into people who hold in their hands only one real asset: the ability to wait.

And I, as a Jew, can understand that well.

"When a person is exiled from his land," a Jewish-American author once said to the Palestinian writer from Ramallah, Raj'a Shehade, "he begins to think of it in symbols, like a person who needs pornography. And we, the Jews, have also become expert pornographers, and our longings for this land are woven of endless symbols." The author was speaking of the Jews of hundreds of

years ago, but on the day I went to Deheisha the Knesset
was storming in fierce debate over the symbolism of the
name "Judea and Samaria," and Knesset member Geula
Cohen demanded that this remain the only legal desig-
nation, and that the terms "West Bank" and "territories" in all their permutations not be used. "Judea and
Samaria" really sounds more significant and symbolical,
and there are many among us for whom the phrase
activates a pleasant historical reflex, a sort of satisfying
shiver reaching into the depths of the past, there spreading ripples of longing for other sleeping phrases as well—
the Bashan, the Gilad, the Horan, all parts of the ancient
Greater Israel and today parts of Syria and Jordan.

About half a million Palestinian refugees live today in
the Gaza Strip. In the West Bank there are about 400,000.
(We are speaking here only of refugees, and not of the
entire Arab population under Israeli rule.) In Jordan
there are about 850,000. In Lebanon, some 250,000.
Syria also has about 250,000. A total of about two and
a quarter million refugees. Even if the problem of the
refugees living under Israeli rule is solved, the bitterness
of their more than a million brothers in the Arab countries, living in no less appalling conditions, will remain.
This is why the feeling of despair is so deep among all
those who know this problem well. This is why the
refugees allow themselves to become addicted to their
dreams.

Raj'a Shehade, writer and lawyer, admits that he, too,
was a pornographer of views in his youth. Of the view
of Jaffa and the coastal plain, about which he has heard
stories and legends. When he hikes today over the hills
next to Ramallah, it happens that he forgets himself for
a minute and he can enjoy the contact with the earth,

smell the thyme, gaze upon an olive tree—and then he
understands that he is looking at an olive tree, and before
his eyes the tree transmutes, and becomes a symbol, the
symbol of struggle, of loss, "and at that very same moment the tree is stolen from me," says Shehade, "and in
its place is a void, filling up with pain and anger."

The void. The absence, which for decades has been
filling with hatred.

A.N., whom I met another time, in Nablus, told me:
"Of course I hate you. Maybe at the beginning I didn't
hate and only feared. Afterwards, I began to hate." A.N.,
thirty years old, is a resident of the Balata refugee camp.
He spent ten years of his life in jail (the Ashkelon and
Nafha prisons) after being found guilty of belonging to
the Popular Front for the Liberation of Palestine. ("I
didn't actually take part in operations. They only taught
me to shoot.") "Before I went to jail, I didn't even know
I was a Palestinian. There they taught me who I am.
Now I have opinions. Don't believe the ones who tell
you that the Palestinians don't really hate you. Understand: the average Palestinian is not the fascist and hating type, but you and the life under your occupation
push him into hatred. Look at me, for example. You
took ten years of my life from me. You exiled my father
in '68. He hadn't done anything. He wasn't even a PLO
supporter. Maybe even the opposite. But you wanted to
kick out anyone who had an opinion about anything.
So that we would be here completely without leaders.
Even without leaders who were a little bit for you. And
my mother—for six years you did not allow her to go
to visit him. And I—after prison, you don't let me build
a house, or leave here to visit Jordan, nothing. And you
constantly repeat: See what progress we have brought

you. You forget that in twenty years everything has progressed. The whole world strides forward. True, you helped us a little, but you aren't willing to give us the most important thing. True, we progressed a little, but look how much you progressed during that time. We remained way behind, and if you check it out, maybe you'll see that we are even worse off in a relative sense than we were in '67." (The standard of living may be measured by personal consumption per capita and GNP per capita. I checked the facts with Dr. Meron Benvenisti, author of *The West Bank Data Project*. In his study, private consumption per capita in the West Bank is estimated at about 30 percent of that of Israel; GNP per capita in the West Bank is four times smaller than in Israel.)

"Then," the young man from Balata continued, restrained in his expression but transmitting cold, tight-lipped anger, "then you say under the Jordanians it was bad for you. Maybe so. But the Jordanians took only our national identity from us, and you took everything. National identity, and the identity of every one of us who fears you and depends on you for his livelihood, you took everything. You made us into living dead. And me, what remains for me? Only the hatred of you and thoughts of *siyassah* [politics]. That's another evil you brought upon us, that you made every man here, even the most ordinary fellah, into a politician."

I drink tea with three women in Deheisha. One hears the most penetrating things from the women. The men are more afraid of imprisonment and intimidation. It is the women who march at the head of the demonstrations, it is the women who shout, who scream out the bitterness in their hearts before the television cameras. Brown women, with sharp features, women bearing suffering. Hadijah is seventy-five years old, her mind sharp and her narrow body healthy. "*Allah yikhalik*," I say to her, may God be with you, and she laughs to herself, a thin chuckle of bare gums, and says: "What is it to him?" and explains to me that a man is like a stalk of wheat: when he turns yellow, he bends.

She has lived in this house, a standard refugee house, for forty years. The United Nations Welfare and Relief Agency (UNWRA) built it, and the UN symbol can still be found on the walls and doors. At the head of each refugee camp in the West Bank and Gaza Strip stands an UNWRA-appointed director. He serves as middleman between the agency and the residents. He is himself a former refugee and lives in the camp. He has the authority to distribute food and welfare payments, to grant the right to live in the camp, and to recommend students for university admissions.

The house consists of two small rooms and does not have running water. The electricity is usually out. Today it is raining outside, and the house is almost completely dark. Hadijah and her elderly sister sit on a straw mat and examine the medicines the camp doctor has prescribed for the sister. She suffers from asthma. The teachers and doctors who work in the refugee camps come, in general, from outside, from the nearby cities. The simplest jobs, cleaning and sanitation and construction, are filled by the camp residents. In the house in which I now sit live five people. In the room in which we drink our tea there is one cabinet, a suitcase on top. Half open. As if waiting to move on. A few wooden chairs made by an untrained hand, a few shelves holding vegetables.

The young woman, tense, offers oranges and a paring knife. Another item of furniture found in every house here is the dowry chest of the woman of the house, made from the soft trunk of the Judas tree. Here she keeps her dowry, the bedsheets, the wedding dress, and perhaps some childish luxury, a toy, a pretty handkerchief—after all, she was no more than a girl when she was married.

"And if someone were to offer you today a dunam [one-quarter acre, the standard measure of land in countries once under Turkish rule] of land in a nice place, with light, in the open air?"

Yes, yes—she laughs—of course, but only on my own land. There.

She also declaims this, like the politicians, like those purveyors of her fate over all these years. She, at least, has the right to do so. I try to remember how many times Palestinian leaders missed opportunities to gain themselves a homeland: there was the partition proposal of '36 and the second proposal of '47, and maybe there were other chances. They—in their blindness—rejected them all. We drink silently. The men are at work. On the wall, two nails. They serve as a wardrobe. On one hangs the black *'igal* (headband) of a kaffiyeh.

Whoever has served in the army in the "territories" knows how such rooms look from the inside during the night. Whoever has taken part in searches, in imposing curfews, in capturing a suspect at night, remembers. The violent entry into rooms like this one, where several people sleep, crowded, in unaired stench, three or four together under scratchy wool blankets, wearing their work clothes still in their sleep, as if ready at any moment to get up and go wherever they are told. They wake in confusion, squinting from the flashlight, children wail, sometimes a couple is making love, soldiers surround the house, some of them—shoes full of mud after tramping through the paths of the camp—walking over the sleep-warm blankets, some pounding on the tin roof above.

The old woman follows, it seems, my gaze to the bare cement walls, the heating lamp, the wool blankets rolled up on the floor. Suddenly she boils over: "Do we look like gypsies, do we? Miserable, are we? Ha? We are people of culture!" Her sister, the sick woman, nods rapidly, her sharp chin stabbing her sunken chest: "Yes, yes, people of culture!" They fall silent, wheezing. The young woman, of the wild, exotic presence, wants to say something and is silent. Her hand literally clamps her mouth closed. Within the arabesque filigree of manners and considered delicacy, of conversation and the protection of hospitality, the wires suddenly go taut. I am confused. The young woman tries to make amends. Change the subject. Is her mother-in-law willing to tell this Israeli here about, for instance, her childhood in Ain Azrab? No. Is she willing to recall the days when she worked the land? No, no. Salt on a wound. Would you be willing, *ya mama*, to sing the songs the fellahin, the winegrowers, the shepherds sang then? No. She only tightens her cracked lips stubbornly, her balding head shaking, but again, out of the conquering power of absence, her left foot begins to tap to a far-off rhythm, and her body moves silently forward and back, and as she traps my cautious gaze, she slaps her thigh with a trembling hand, and her nose reddens with rage: "Culture! You people don't know that we have culture! You can't understand this culture. It's not a culture of television!"

Suddenly she is completely emptied of her anger: once again her face takes on an expression of defeat, of knowing all, the ancient signs written on the faces of the old: "The world is hard, hard . . ." She nods her head in bitter sorrow, her eyes close themselves off from the small, dark room: "You can't understand. You can't understand anything. Ask, maybe, your grandmother to tell you."

2

I Want to

Shoot Jews

Again in Deheisha. It is a quiet day today. No demonstrations. No stone throwing. The army can be seen only from afar, riding along the road. A week later there would be riots and demonstrations and rocks would fly, and around Deheisha would rise a six-meter fence, to prevent stones from being thrown on every passing car. Deheisha would become invisible as far as the travelers along the road were concerned, and the fence would become, it seems, a new Palestinian symbol. The rainwater and the sewage still flow in rivulets along the paths. A man lays a heavy stone on a tin roof to prevent the wind from blowing it away. A group of young men build another room onto a house. They are building everywhere here. With determination and without any plan. "Why is Thekla's construction taking such a long time?" Marco Polo asked the hardworking builders in Italo Calvino's book *Invisible Cities*, and they answered him—without pausing for a moment from lifting pails and moving their long brushes up and down: "So that its destruction cannot begin." Do you fear that the minute you take down the scaffolding the city will begin to crumble and fall to pieces? And the residents of the invisible city answered hastily, in a whisper: "Not only the city."

The owner of the little grocery store is surprised at my entry, and rises in concern. The merchandise is scanty and old. For the most part it consists of cigarettes, soft drinks, and cans of pineapple displaying suntanned young women covered with dust. Why bother describing it? We are all acquainted with a store just like it. The storeowner's friend, Abu Hana, checks first to see if I am not from the *mukhabarat*, the intelligence service, and afterwards says that he will speak of anything except bolitics, since bolitics is a science in which it is very difficult to discover anything new, no?

Yes, it would seem.

It is better to remain silent, he says. Then he finds that he cannot hold back, and sounds a hurried whisper: "Napoleon, Bismarck, Hitler," he says. "None of them lasted. They were too strong. It's best to sit quietly and wait."

Wait for what?

I don't know. I'm no genius. What do I know?

And he smiles me a calculated, distancing smile.

I look him over. An Arab dressed in a kaffiyeh and enveloped in a neutral, purposeful expression, against the background of a strongly lined face, engraved by a harsh hand. The bank clerk who told me a week ago, in the voice of one making me party to a secret, "I most hate working on the tenth of the month, when all the *arabushim* get their pay," was thinking, no doubt, of this *arabush*. Or maybe she meant the other *arabushim*, who also wear a mask of ignorance and apathy, to the point that the mask has seeped into their skins.

And on the slope of the hill in Deheisha, I passed a group of small children racing upward. *Rowda*. An Arab kindergarten. Two teachers (Don't give our names, but you can quote) and thirty-five children from two to five years old. The Deheisha kindergarten.

I want to expand a little on this subject: the small children, nameless, with running noses, the ones we see along the roads, playing by the passing cars. These are the children who in '67 sold us figs for a *grush* and washed our parents' cars for ten *grush*. And afterwards they grew up a little and became the *shbab*, you know, the ones with the look of hate in their eyes, rioting in the streets and throwing stones at our soldiers, tying a lasso to the crown of a cypress tree, bending it to the ground, attaching a Palestinian flag to it, and freeing the tree—and you, the soldier, go cut down the moon; and afterwards they grew a little more, and from among them came the ones who make the Molotov cocktails and the bombs. They are the same children from '67. Nothing has changed in the refugee camps, and their future is etched on their faces like an ancient, fossilized record.

For now, they are little children in kindergarten. One group shouts and cheers, and after making a conscious effort—necessary, perhaps, for all strangers and for Jews and Israelis in particular—I begin to differentiate their faces, their voices, their smiles, their characters, and slowly also their beauty and delicacy, and this is not easy. It requires an investment of energy on my part, since I also have trained myself to look at Arabs with that same blurred vision which makes it easier for me (only for me?) to deal with their chiding, accusing, threatening presence, and during this month of encounters with them I must do exactly the opposite, enter the vortex of my greatest fear and repulsion, direct my gaze at the invisible Arabs, face this forgotten reality, and see how—as in the process of developing a picture—it emerges before me slowly, slowly from the emulsion in the darkroom of my fears and my sublimations.

The teachers? They giggle, they blush, they consult each other: yes. They would be happy to take me to see their kindergarten. We stride upward between the boulders and the puddles. In every direction, someone is busy building. Renovating. Painting. The families are large, and more and more must be built. "Where is the plan you are following, the blueprint?" Italo Calvino's Marco Polo asked the citizens of Thekla, and received no answer until night fell and the star-filled heavens were spread above. "There is the blueprint," they answered him.

And on the roof of one of those houses sits a boy, twelve years old perhaps, head shaved and eyes closed, and he plays devotedly on a comb wrapped in paper. Fiddler on the roof.

Between two buildings sits a cement structure, plastered white on the outside. Closed with an iron door on which is the UNWRA emblem. It looks like a public bomb shelter from the fifties. The young teacher opens the iron door, filled with holes, and I enter the Deheisha kindergarten.

First, one has to get used to the dimness. There is no electricity in the kindergarten. I stand in a long, narrow space, divided into two rooms. There is not one picture on the grayish walls; because of the dampness, the wall crumbles if you try to pound a nail into it. In the corner of the room, a metal table and two chairs. And one other piece of furniture: a thin reed mat.

The teacher tells the children to sit, and they do so, crowding onto the mat. They chatter with each other, as children do, until the teacher tells them to be quiet. From that moment on, they are totally silent, not making a sound during the entire conversation. In an Israeli kindergarten the children are unable to remain quiet for a single minute. They jump up from their places, run to the teacher, say what they have to say, argue. They are free children, and you can understand what this blessed, natural freedom is only when you see its opposite. "The children here are so quiet and disciplined," I said to the kindergarten teacher in Deheisha, and she answered with an Arabic proverb: "The gosling floats like the gander"—like father, like son.

"Where are you from?"
"From Zakaria. A village."
"Were you born there?"

She laughs. Really. Even her mother has no memories from there. Mother was five years old when they fled. It is Grandmother who preserves the family tradition. Grandmother, married at the age of seven to a twenty-year-old man. This is what happened: the Turkish Army was at the gates of the country, and the Arabs feared that the Turkish soldiers would take the girls. So they betrothed them while they were still in diapers. Grandfather himself went out to the Great War, and when he returned once on furlough his little wife called him a bad name. He became angry with her, lifted her up in his hands, and threw her far away. That's how little she was!

And the giggly kindergarten teacher bends over with laughter as she tells the story. Today that grandmother has four sons and a daughter in Deheisha. She has survived the Turks, the British, the Jordanians, and the Israelis—four occupations.

She is attractive, the ruddy-cheeked teacher, and looks the way our high-school girls once looked. That anarchist enthusiasm of youth. She is sharp and excitable, and is not afraid to say what is on her mind. She was born in Deheisha, and she supposes she will spend her whole life here. She is engaged to a young man from the camp. How do they enjoy themselves? There isn't much to do here, she answers, we go to friends, to relatives. Even after the wedding, the couple has no place to be alone.

"Where will you build your house?"

"In the camp, over my parents' house."

"And you don't want to leave here for a better place?"

"Only for my homeland. Even if they offer me a palace. Our parents made a mistake when they left their homes. We won't make that mistake."

"And you don't dream sometimes, only dream, that you might live in a better place?"

"Dreams?" She laughs. "I have a responsibility," she says, "to the suffering my parents endured, and to my own suffering."

"And because of responsibility to suffering you won't try to achieve even limited possible happiness?"

"I can't. I don't want to."

"And who will help you return to your village—Arafat?"

"Arafat? Arafat is bourgeois. He drives a Mercedes. He doesn't feel the suffering of the refugees. All the Fatah commanders have houses in Syria and the Gulf states. Arafat has no supporters here. Only we can represent ourselves."

"And if Arafat achieves a political settlement? There is talk now of an international conference, you know."

"Understand. We are against Arafat, because Arafat wants peace. We want a solution by force. What was taken by force will be returned by force. Only thus."

Only thus. I remember the similarity between the symbol of the Irgun and that of the PLO: here a fist grasping a rifle against a map of the land of Israel, and there two fists, holding rifles, against the very same map.

The young and enthusiastic kindergarten teacher was neither the first nor the last person I met during these weeks who voluntarily turned himself into an object, a play toy in the hands of those dealers in life and death, into an impersonal symbol. Into a collective noun. When I stand before such people, I have no idea where to begin unraveling this web of iron.

"And the children, what about them?" I ask.

"The children here know everything," she says, and her friend nods. "Some of the children here are the fourth generation in the camp. On any night the army may enter their house, right into the house, conduct a search, shout, turn over the blankets and slash at them with their bayonets, strip their fathers—here, Naji here—"

Naji is two and a half years old, short for his age, black eyes, curls.

"A month ago they took his father, and he doesn't know where he is, or if he will ever return."

"A little while ago," says the second teacher, somewhat heavy, blue-eyed, and delicately made up, always on the edge of a giggle or a blush, "a little while ago the military governor visited the kindergarten and asked if I teach the children bad things, against Israel and the Jews."

"And what did you say to him?"

"I said that I don't. But that his soldiers do."

"What do you mean?"

"What do I mean? I'll explain. When a child goes for a walk outside and sees a tree, he knows that the tree bears fruit and leaves, right? When he sees a soldier, he knows very well what that soldier does. Do you understand?"

"What do soldiers do?" I ask a girl of about four, called Naima, green-eyed, little gold earrings in her ears.

"Searches and beatings."

"Do you know who the Jews are?"

"The army."

"Are there other Jews?"

"No."

"What does your father do?"

"Sick."

"And your mother?"

"She works in Jerusalem for the Jews. Cleans their houses."

So she answers me, the new little Palestinian problem.

"And you"—a chubby boy, somewhat dreamy— "do you know who the Jews are?"

"Yes. They took my sister."

"Where to?"

"To Farah."

(Both his sisters are there, in jail, the teachers explain.)

"What did your sisters do?"

"They did *not* throw stones," he says angrily.

Suddenly a little boy gets up, holding a short yellow plastic stick in his hand, and shoots me.

"Why are you shooting me?"

He runs to the teacher, peeks at me from behind her arm, and laughs. He is two years old.

"Who do you want to shoot?" the teachers ask, smiling, like two mothers taking pride in a smart child.

"Jews."

Their lips make out the answer with him.

"Now tell him why," they encourage the little one.

"Because the Jews took my uncle," he says. "At night they came in and stole him from the bed, so now I sleep with my mother all the time."

"Is this the answer, to bring up another generation and another in hatred? To teach them that this hatred justifies the refusal to work toward a solution? Couldn't you try, maybe, another way?"

"There is no other way," they answer, both of them, each in her own way, in a whisper or with self-assurance, but the same words.

I stand and listen and try to be neutral. To understand. Not to judge. And also not to be like an American or French correspondent, completely severed from the whole complex of events, and quick to pass judgment. But I also stand here as a reserve soldier in the Israeli Army, and as a human being, rising up against this education in blind hatred, and against such tremendous energy being expended for the preservation of malice, instead of being spent in an effort to get out of this barrenness, this ugliness in which this kindergarten lies, these little children who are so good at hating me.

A boy raises his hand. Needs to make peepee. I accompany him. The bathroom is only a little niche separated from the room by a curtain. In its center, a hole in the ground and a porcelain platter. Little piles of excrement all over, and the urinating boy steps in some. I remember the textbooks full of hate and anti-Israel propaganda found by Israeli soldiers twenty years ago, after the war, in the schools and kindergartens. Those books were confiscated, but their content is now transmitted orally. The oral law. It doesn't matter at all who is really guilty of the refugee camps—we, the Israelis, will pay the price. We, and not the Arab countries or the world. It is us they will hate, these children living their whole lives in a colorless world without happiness, who spend long summer and winter hours in a cold and mildewed kindergarten, which has neither a glass window nor electricity. With the all-pervading stink rising from the "bathroom" a grotesque symbol of their situation.

"What games do you play here?"

"Games like everywhere," says the younger teacher. "Tag. Hide-and-seek. There are toys, too."

Two small cardboard boxes hold the kindergarten's toys: old, faded toys. Someone's donation. Not one toy is whole. None of the cars has wheels. Dolls have missing limbs. There is no mercy.

They also have songs, the kindergarten children in Deheisha. The teachers stand them in a line. "What do we sing when the army goes by? One, two, three, four!" And the children break out in song:

"We went out into the street/We waved the flags/We sang for our country the nicest of songs/a song of freedom and unity/a song of victory through struggle/Bloom, my land/By throwing stones and burning tires we will free the motherland . . ."

I recall the Jewish children who sang patriotic songs

when British soldiers passed by. They must also have felt like heroes when they did. It is always the same play, only the players change, and sometimes the roles. It requires a lot of strength to change roles, adapt, learn new lines, inure yourself to the complex significance of the new part.

"And jokes about us," I ask them, as if I am not at all part of the joke, "do you tell jokes about us?"

They think for a minute, astounded that there aren't any. There really aren't. No jokes at all? No slang expression, twenty years old, to describe the border guards, the Shin Bet (the secret security service), the military governor?

We, says the smiling teacher, laugh mostly at ourselves.

Strange that they have no jokes about us. In other places I received the same answer. Really, they asked themselves, how is it that there aren't any jokes? It would be interesting to examine what they do with all that aggression and hatred of us. Who is their Sholem Aleichem? Is it that they unconsciously avoid seeking an outlet in humor? Do they prefer to preserve their hatred and humility unworked, raw, and wild?

"I don't tell the children bad things about Israel," the heavy one says, and adjusts her sweater, "but I tell them stories, stories about animals," she hints.

Like fables.

". . . like, for example, there were small sparrows on a terebinth tree, playing and having a good time, and suddenly came a cruel black raven who coveted their tree and expelled them from it. They were very sad. They almost died of sorrow, until they got up and gathered together, and flew against him as a great and united group, and so were able to expel him from their tree."

"You made it up?"

"Yes. I have a few stories like that. The children already understand."

"And did they succeed in organizing themselves together, the birds?"

"Yes. They are very wise. They're birds, not Palestinians."

Toward evening I travel to Jerusalem. The roads are lined with rusty cars. Metal ruins, tires stuck on barbed-wire fences, old hot-water tanks, discarded doors, walls dirtied with half-erased graffiti, old shoes . . . everything left bare and harsh along the road, everything preserved, awakening pent-up melancholy: all this abandoned, like a rebellion and cry against a destroyed, corrupt, irreparable circumstance.

At six in the evening I arrive at the Ben Yehuda mall in downtown Jerusalem to buy *Dear Brothers*, a book about the Jewish underground by one of its members, Haggai Segel. The evening is gray and misty, and the people are burdened with their civilian matters, isolated so much from the hate and the danger, as I walked among them like the bearer of evil tidings among the unaware. In the thin fog and with the light of the yellow streetlamps it is possible to succumb to illusions and see behind every person a halo, a sort of double peeking out for a split second, the identical twin of this man, his double from Nablus, and that young woman, whose unknown twin I met this morning at Deheisha, that same walk and same smile and same quiet sensuality, and for every child there was a double, and none of them knew, and none of them guessed a thing.

3

What the
Arabs Dream

What do the Arabs dream about? And what do Jewish children dream about? Is it possible to hope that the dreams of the Jews and the Arabs provide some sort of escape and easing and refinement of the harsh and cruel reality of life—or are dreams only a direct continuation of it?

And why should the mirror mold of dreams not create some sort of closeness, a dialogue unknown to its participants, anti-grammar, unexpectedly creating a new language?

It will not happen.

Dr. Yoram Bilu, a lecturer in psychology at the Hebrew University of Jerusalem, examined with the help of his students, Yussuf Nashef and Tehila Blumenthal, the dreams of eleven-to-thirteen-year-old children in different parts of Israel and the West Bank. Part of his study concerned the children of the Kalandia refugee camp, and the children of Gush Etzion and Kiryat Arba, Jewish settlements in the West Bank.

Every child who took part in the study received a

colored notebook and was asked to record four dreams immediately upon wakening. The age of the subjects was fixed so that they would be old enough to write down their dreams but not old enough to be bothered by sexual dreams.

And one other important comment: the children in the refugee camp did not know that the study was for the Hebrew University. The notebooks were given to them through UNWRA and afterwards were carefully translated. What dreams do they dream?

Seventeen percent of the dreams of the Jewish children dealt with meetings with Arabs. (To the attention of those who wish at any price to prevent such meetings. And by the way: does the law recently passed by the Knesset making it illegal for Israelis to meet with PLO members include dream meetings? Check.) In contrast, 30 percent of the children in the Kalandia refugee camp dreamed during the brief period of the study at least one dream involving some sort of meeting with a Jew. The meaning of this, according to Dr. Bilu, is that the children in the Kalandia camp "are obsessively involved with the conflict."

But whom exactly do Jews and Arabs meet on moonless nights?

Among 328 dreams of meetings (Jews and Arabs) there is not one character identified by name. There is not a single figure defined by a personal, individual appearance. All the descriptions, without exception, are completely stereotyped; the characters defined only by their ethnic identification (Jew, Arab, Zionist, etc.) or by value-laden terms with negative connotations (the terrorists, the oppressors, etc.). The Arabs do not try to refine their stereotyped characters. The Jews make some sort of effort—in general, the word "Arab" is associated for them with the word "criminal." "I lived in an Arab city, full of criminals," wrote an eleven-year-old from Kiryat Arba. "I entered the grocery store and two men, an Arab and a gangster, attacked me there," dreamed another boy from the same town. "We have to educate the Arabs, so that they will be good, law-abiding citizens," declared another young citizen from among the Jewish settlers in Hebron. "I taught them to write in Hebrew, until they became good people, and then they freed them from the jail, and they didn't make any more problems."

The Arabs often find escape in apocalyptic dreams, in which the final, decisive battle is held, and the Arab armies, dressed in shining white, are ranged against the Jewish heretics, wrapped in black. The battle is always won by the good guys.

Jewish children also have trouble facing the constant struggle, offering no escape, and they find release in imagination and transference: Kiryat Arba children told, for example, of a colored flying saucer which landed on the border between Israel and "the land of the enemy"; of soldiers from Uganda who attacked a Jewish child, and a twelve-year-old went the farthest when he dreamed that he was walking, minding his own business, in the heart of Hebron and was cruelly attacked from the back, "and I turned around and managed to see that it was a Chinese boy . . ."

The majority of the interactions in the dreams are violent and aggressive and end in death. The dreams of the children of the Kalandia refugee camp indicate a hard and threatening reality, a fragile world with no defense. The typical "plot" of such a dream is played out in the camp: the boundaries of the dreamer's house are very permeable, nothing provides him with defense and security, strange people invade the house and attack the child. Frequently, they torture him to death. His parents are unable to protect him. One dream in particular caught my eye: "The Zionist Army surrounds our house and breaks in. My big brother is taken to prison and is tortured there. The soldiers continue to search the house. They throw everything around, but do not find the person they want [the dreamer himself]. They leave the house, but return, helped by a treacherous neighbor. This time they find me and my relatives, after we had all hidden in the closet in fright."

The Holocaust appears in many dreams of the Kiryat Arba children. An eleven-year-old girl writes: "My friend and I decided to go to Jericho. Suddenly we heard someone calling us from behind. They were my parents. They said that I have to take off the yellow star I was wearing. The star is a large yellow piece of paper, showing that we support the partisans. The city, Jericho, was against the partisans. But it turned out that my friend and I had taken off the star too late, because suddenly someone came, took us to a grove of trees, and ordered us to crawl on the ground along with many other people. Crawling, we reached a tunnel, but only my father was allowed to enter, and my mother and I had to continue to the place for the women. Suddenly I saw something move: it was an old woman starting out of her grave. Her face was covered with earth."

Guilt feelings appear only among the Jewish children. So, for instance, in the dream of a twelve-year-old girl from Kiryat Arba: ". . . suddenly someone grabs me, and I see that it is happening in my house, but my family went away, and Arab children are walking through our rooms, and their father holds me, he has a kaffiyeh and his face is cruel, and I am not surprised that it is happening, that these Arabs now live in my house. I accept that as if that is the way it is supposed to be."

It is a long and detailed study, but it seems to me that these few examples are sufficient. The dreams offer neither escape nor relief. There are no moments of pity and no friendly contact. Some of them are nightmares, difficult to read, and more difficult to realize the price being paid by our children and the Arab children for living in this conflict. This conflict, from which there is no escape even in dreams.

The writer J. M. Coetzee, who also lives in a cruel land, complex to the point of being almost insoluble, recently received the Jerusalem Prize; in his speech he recalled the philosopher Nietzsche, who said: "We have art so that we shall not die of reality." "In South Africa," Coetzee said, "there is now too much truth for the art to hold. Truth that overwhelms and swamps every act of the imagination."

Among us, even dreams are crushed under the weight of reality.

One fact is particularly interesting, concerning what does *not* appear in this study: among some thousand dreams of Jewish and Arab children, there is not one which indicates a longing for peace.

4

Don't Pity Them
Too Much

"Let me put it this way," said Jabo at the end of the evening in Ofra. "We conducted a debate here, and we think you lost. But you've got the stronger hand, because you can write it any way you want."

Given the challenge and the heavy responsibility which Jabo placed in my hands, I mean to write cautiously, step by step, and perhaps in doing so I can return the challenge to the people of Ofra, so that they may face up to the implications of what they told me.

For the stranger, the wary, the visitor from afar, Ofra surprises. On Friday afternoon it is soft and green, accessible and unfenced, and its people are welcoming, warm, and unassuming. Quickly, so quickly, the wary stranger is also seduced by the ethereal sense of festivity that permeates the Sabbath here, and in wonder he discovers in himself a tender desire to be absorbed in it in his entirety, to let down his guard, to become worthy of this welcome, of this nostalgic flickering of the candle flame awaiting him at the end of the rough road between the villages of Ain Yabrud and Silwad.

I did not want to make a short visit to Ofra. I wanted an extended one, a weekend, to see the people of this place at all hours of the day, unguarded. With their children. On a typical street I looked for the home of the family which would host me, and found it between, on the one side, the houses of Yehuda Etzion and Yitzhak Novick, and on the other, of Haggai Segel, all members of the terrorist Jewish underground, arrested three years ago. Its members were convicted variously of booby-trapping the cars of the mayors of four West Bank cities, of killing two students and wounding several others in an attack on the Islamic college in Hebron, of planting bombs in Arab buses, and of conspiring to blow up the Dome of the Rock, the Moslem shrine which sits on the site of the ancient Jewish Temple. I stayed, with my family, in the home of Menahem and Na'ama Granit and their four children, warm and pleasant people. The people of Gush Emunim, of the settlements, are used to hosting wary strangers like myself. "We never know when we will get a phone call announcing that tomorrow five or six guests are coming for a meal, for an entire day, for Shabbat," related Ayala Resis-Tal. "Welcome. We're used to it." Gush Emunim, currently somewhat moribund because of the lack of widespread new settlement activity; also as a result of the exposure of the Jewish underground and the sharp internal debates which that event brought on, puts much effort into disseminating its ideas, bringing people closer to its values, and bringing its interests into the public eye. Its publicity machine is well oiled, to the point where you almost don't notice you are being "sold" something, and only afterwards realize that the people here do not listen much, do not display a real interest in you, and that two- and three-hour heart-to-heart conversations revolve, in the end, exclusively around them and their lives. This, perhaps, is the first warning sign of the price they pay.

As for the debate:

To begin with, I did not intend to debate at all, and I don't see that evening—in the book-lined study of Rav Yoel Ben-Nun—as a debate. Furthermore, at the end of twenty years it seems to me that all the arguments, both rational and emotional, have already been made. Only on extremely rare occasions do we hear a crushing new argument, one which requires you to reevaluate your opinions, and in Israel the reality is that it is easier for a man to change his religion, and maybe even his sex, than to change in any decisive way his political opinions. Renounce your opinions—and it is as if you have announced the total replacement of the structure of your soul, and have taken it upon yourself to proclaim that, up to now, you lived a perfect lie. So each bunker peers with its periscope at the bunker across the way, and sees there the reflection of the shining iron of its own immovability. So much for debate.

But debate was, it seems, inevitable. It began in this way: I opened by explaining what I was doing there, in Ofra, on Shabbat. What I came for and what I wanted to hear. I told of my meetings with Arabs in the area, of the pent-up (how appropriate an adjective!) hatred I found among some of them; I told of my visits to the refugee camps. Someone immediately remonstrated—as if by conditioned reflex: Don't pity them too much. Haven't you seen their mansions along the road to Ramallah?

I said that I had seen them, and other things as well, and that I hadn't come to hold forth on that subject.

The Ofrans leaned forward in their chairs. From that moment they lost the peacefulness of the Sabbath eve, and an invisible trip wire joined them all, facing me. I thought that there was no point in contention. They have lived in the middle of the conflict for so many years, trained to resist any attack, justified or unjustified, lacking in their naked vulnerability any sense of irony.

For this reason, and instead of answering, I asked for their goodwill. For their cooperation in one matter that bothers me. A side question, not even part of the debate over who is more in the right, we or the Arabs. The right or the left. Because I am very curious to see if they can imagine themselves in their Arab neighbors' places and tell me what seems to them to be the most hateful manifestation of the occupation.

Someone (it is difficult to remember who, there were about fifty people there) said immediately, "The situation isn't our fault!" And others murmured their agreement.

I said: That is not the question. Let's assume that you are right. Let us assume that your view is correct one hundred percent, and that history will confirm this in time. Now I ask only for a little flexibility of thought, and ask again: What, in your opinions, does an Arab in Silwad or Ain Yabrud, in his everyday life, in his most private meditations, in his relations with his children, in what does he most feel the influence of your (just, you believe) presence here, in a place he sees as his land.

"We haven't taken one meter of land from Arabs," one woman said heatedly.

I saw that I had erred and not made myself clear. So I told them how I describe this to myself, and permit me to record it here with a certain lack of modesty: I related that in my own day-to-day life I attach extremely great importance to time. That sometimes I feel as if time flows in my veins. And I am not willing to tolerate the thought that even one moment of my life might pass empty of meaning, of interest, of enjoyment. I feel great responsibility to the time given us with such meanness, and it seems to me that, were I living under foreign rule, what would torture me would be—besides the tangible things that are taken as given—the fact that I do not control my time. That they can delay me at a roadblock for an hour-long interrogation; that they can impose a curfew of several days on me; that the hours of my life, which are my personal, intimate possession, turn into worn coins in the hands of a wasteful and obtuse malevolence. And this also: that they set me at an unnatural point in the general progress of historical time; that they hold back or accelerate developments and processes in an artificial and arbitrary way, without my being able to make use of all that is inherent in them. And I returned to my now familiar question.

"Fine," said one of the Ofrans. "At the intersection coming into Tel Aviv I also get held up an hour every morning."

Laughter.

"To my mind time is so valuable," said my host, "that I don't waste even a minute on such questions."

More laughter.

But now I was not willing to give up, because it seemed to me that this was an expression of a fundamental and deep difficulty. So, for forty minutes, I continued to ask the same question over and over, and the Ofrans, educated, sharp-minded, and fluent as they are, did not succeed in answering my question, my simple request.

Erlich said that what most burdens the Arabs is actually our, the Jews', indecision with regard to the situation, and that, were we to decide to officially annex the territories, we would make things easier for them. That's an answer to a different question, I said. The atmosphere had already become unpleasant.

Haggai Segel's father stood in the doorway opposite me, erect, wearing a black beret, and his face expressed his hostility toward me. He stated angrily that we did not start the war (absolutely right) and that we won a victory over all our enemies in an almost miraculous way (true), and what do you think, that now we can give up everything we gained. I thought only that this also did not answer that earlier, forgotten question.

Among the myriad arguments thrown at me (sometimes by two or three voices in unison) were some which indicated an attempt to deal with the question. Noga spoke of the Bedouin she saw on television a month earlier, an Israeli Bedouin from near Beersheba, who could not find work and felt himself to be a second-class citizen. Gidele said that he is not comfortable with the way soldiers at roadblocks treat Arabs, and that he even tells them so. These were not real answers, but they showed a willingness to consider the question. Other than these and one or two other responses, the people in the room were not able, even for a little while, to shift their point of view; they did not allow themselves even a split second of empathy and uncommitted participation in the lives of those whose fates are intertwined and interwoven so much with theirs. Like fossils, they did not succeed in freeing themselves from those very bonds which they are unwilling to admit exist.

Then Yehuda said that the answer is simple: that he

does not want to think even for a minute about the situation of the Arabs around him, because he is caught up in a struggle with them, at war, he said, and were he to allow himself to pity, to identify, he would weaken and endanger himself. The people in the room nodded. There was a hum of agreement.

I said that such an answer—even though anticipated—frightens me, because there are things that, when said out loud, become both a judgment and a prophecy. After such things are said out loud, is it possible to say that twenty years of heart-hardening have had no side effects?

"We've heard that kind of talk before," the Ofrans said. I was not sure they had really listened. I expanded on my question a bit more, not only for them, but also to understand it better myself: when we wish to ignore someone, some other person, or thousands of people, we set up a sort of "block" in our souls. A closed-off area, fencing in all the problems we do not wish to touch. Little by little we learn to make detours, to distance ourselves from that same closed area. Our access to it is blocked. Without our noticing, it ceases to be ours. Something is lost and taken away from us, maybe forever. We are social creatures, I told the people of Ofra, and even when we are completely alone we create internal relationships with different parts of ourselves. And when we accustom ourselves to relations like those between master and slave, that division is stamped within us as well. It suddenly becomes a possible mold for our relations with our friends.

The charge most often leveled at you of Gush Emunim is approximately this: Can a person spend years closed off from and insensitive to "certain kinds" of people whom he sees face-to-face every day, without this finding its way into other parts of his life? You probably, by this time, don't hear the charge. You have accustomed yourselves to it, and those who made it have grown tired of it themselves. So it is necessary to pain you even more and ask you: Is the soul a modular mechanism in which specific "parts" may be disconnected, or in which entire sections may be made non-operational for a period of time, in the meanwhile, until the danger passes? Can it be—and this each one of us must answer himself, alone— that in the very making of this dramatic separation you do not turn yourself, in the course of time, into just such an impenetrable mechanism, a mechanism that you sometimes control and that sometimes controls you and is capable of deeds that once were only imagined but today are already—

And I said "the Jewish underground," and they answered me yes, yes, the underground, they always throw the underground at us. And in the same breath, almost, they began to attack my hypocrisy, since I live in Talpiot, which, they claimed, used to be an Arab neighborhood, and I do not make an issue of that, and is that not a sin against absolute justice?

I answered that the person who seeks absolute justice is evading practical decisions, and that I do not seek pure justice, nor the settling of historical accounts, but rather possible life, no more than imperfect and tolerable, causing as little injustice as possible. "And Talpiot?" they pressured me, like victors. "What about Talpiot?" I noted that they were mistaken—Talpiot was never an Arab neighborhood, and that in any case I cannot be responsible for what was done before I was born, and that on the contrary, since today we see the results of earlier wars, we must take care not to bring about further injustice. They speak, I said, as if nothing had happened between 1948 and 1967, no developments, no processes, no Green Line—the border between the State of Israel and the West Bank. They talk as if everything is undetermined and unbounded, everything happening in some sort of vacuum, outside of history, and the debate caught fire, the atmosphere became unfriendly, and we had to decide to meet again, the next day, "to talk about literature and not politics," and in order to make up and get over the resentment.

No one today doubts that the people of Gush Emunim have distanced themselves greatly from the center of the Israeli consensus. At the beginning they meant—under the inspiration of Rav Tzvi Yehuda Kook—"to exalt the soul of the nation" by virtue of their deeds over the Green Line, and to draw after them the entire nation to the land of the forefathers to a new system of values, as in the words of the Song of Songs, "Draw me, and we will run after you," but the condition they set themselves was to be "two steps ahead of the nation"—and no more.

But in their haste they raced forward and were left without troops and without support. Without even the favor of many who at the start thought well of them. It is enough to read any issue of their magazine *Nekudah* to realize this. "The settlers developed a feeling of persecution as a defense mechanism, similar to what was essential in its time to the Jewish nation in exile for its defense and adjustment to an inimical environment," writes clinical psychologist and Gush Emunim member Tzvi Moses. "The existence of such a mechanism in the psyche of the Jewish nation creates a problematic system in which change is difficult, and which may be destructive first and foremost to whoever feels persecuted, even though the aggression is, on the surface, directed against the critical and attacking object . . . Obstinacy and inflexible thinking typify the campaigns of the Gush today . . . There are side effects, such as excessive and nostalgic preoccupation with the early days of the movement, and difficulty making necessary adjustments . . . What today typifies the elders of the Gush—those same people who pushed for quick achievements at the start—is that they have revealed themselves to be functionaries fearful that control will be taken out of their hands, so they retard the organization's normal development processes . . . In fear of the dynamic of change, necessary for growth and development, there is excessive and repeated use of ideological concepts, to the point where they are eroded and emptied of meaning. What has happened to those who have grown tired of the slogans of the left about 'democracy' and 'rule of law' is now happening to those who have tired of the unceasing and overworked expressions 'the people of Israel' and 'the land of Israel.' All difficulties and internal mishaps are blamed on outside forces: the government, the left, the Arabs. There is no self-examination of functioning." (*Nekudah* 108, March 1987)

Because of this self-distancing of Gush Emunim from the central consensus, and mostly because of the underground, the general public has become estranged and hesitant with regard to its members and is reluctant to face up to the problem they present. They are frozen into a tired stereotype, and there are those who fear them in an almost mythic way: "You're going to Ofra? Be careful of them" was the reaction of some people when they heard where I was going; and "They're crazy. They're fanatics. They're blind."

It is obvious, however, that it is not so simple, and that reality never surrenders to a stereotypic view. So I went in order to learn.

Perhaps there are not among them real moderates, but there are those who feel growing discomfort. Like those who in private conversations will finally agree to acknowledge the qualms awakening in them over what they are doing to the Arabs and to the people of Israel. There are people here such as Yoel Ben-Nun, rabbi and thinker, who sees the conflict in a wide historical perspective, and whose ideas are thought-provoking and present a real challenge. I do not want to begin listing the many other names, but I met in Ofra men and women who—when calm—are very different from the public image of them. Sensitive, deep people who stimulate thought and fondness. But again—when calm. Even then it is hard to really get to know them. Theirs is a closed society with a clear internal code of its own, of people with, in general, very similar biographies, interacting with each other over a course of years, people who have been molded since childhood by the same common experiences and struggles. The people I met are diligent, idealistic, and without a doubt courageous and ready to sacrifice themselves. Among themselves they maintain a system of mutual assistance and a high level of ideological and personal obligation. Ofra even became the model of a new type of settlement—neither a cooperative agricultural village nor an impersonal town, like those previously established, but a "community settlement," a small, selective community of independent settlers, most of whom run businesses or work in the city.

Despite this, they are not the elite they like to think they are. In conversations with them, one wonders at the extent to which their way of thinking is sometimes simplistic, provincial, nourished by generations of suspicious self-confinement from the world. Conservatism, an important value in their eyes, disconnects them even more from the world around them and strengthens the "bunker" mentality, and it is hard to know whether they hate this or whether it is essential to their continued survival and faith.

In their conversation and their writing they unhesitatingly make use of empty clichés full of baseless arrogance ("We must move the ship of Zionism forward," Daniella Weiss, Secretary-General of Gush Emunim, said). They speak of themselves as being "a model society," but all their actions already give evidence of, on the one hand, weariness of the model life (and there is already hidden competition over the interior and exterior beautification of the private houses and over the number of electrical appliances they contain), and one may also sense among them, on the other hand, a certain perplexity when they must deal with the little details of everyday life, with long-range actions, since, as Ofra educator Dan Tor said, the nucleus of people which created the "Gush Emunim momentum" was "a group with *'high messianic tension'* " (*Dear Brothers*, p. 219). This tension is diffusing itself. And the tension will want release.

The members of Gush Emunim would like to see themselves as the heirs of the historic Mapai (Labor) movement (and the elders of Mapai never hid their sentimental softheartedness in the face of the adventures of the new pioneers of Zionism), but they do not have an

inclusive and deep national vision with "appeal" and
wide public support, as Mapai, the predecessor of today's Labor Party, had in its heyday. They have too few
great lights, and they rally around them in a rough sort
of way, like the inhabitants of a poor Galician town
drawing pride and courage from its local celebrated
scholar.

They accuse the left of having an exile mentality, but
they are not themselves really of the land of Israel. The
architecture of their villages is strange to the landscape,
proud and overbearing; they know nothing of the language, thinking, or manners of their neighbors; among
many of them even the Hebrew language is incorrect,
shallow, and trite. Their houses are almost bookless,
with the exception of religious texts, and, in general,
they have little use for culture. Even the humor of their
circles is of the old Diaspora type, of sarcasm and con-
trariety, and reflexive, nervous contrivances, of mocking
one's real and imagined enemies. The whole world is
against us, they broadcast to you with every word. Inevitably, they have created their own prison, their spiritual
Sparta on the mountaintops, out of which they peek,
stiff and prickly, in the face of all other opinions. They
turned from people of faith to, if one translates the name
Gush Emunim, a Bloc of the Faithful.

Who are these people, I ask myself, who maintain an
almost utopian bubble of a society of values, making
great demands on individuals, atop a mountain of injustice, impenetrability, and ignorance of their fellow
men?

They have established an exemplary settlement here,
among the Arab villages. Both good air and a good life.
They are fruitful and multiply, and there are many fam-

ilies of four, six, and eight children, *kein ein hara*, and a school for five hundred children, an absorption center for new immigrants, cherry orchards and chicken coops—and of all this I do not write, because there is something else, difficult and threatening and much more important, somewhere under it all, which I want to unearth.

No: they are not hotheaded. It is their complexity that is dangerous, not their simplistic willingness to follow their slogans. They plan their steps with wisdom, in a calculated and pragmatic way. In this sense they are utopian rather than messianic. They are not sleepwalking hallucinators but, rather, very practical people.

When you sit with them, especially with the moderates among them, whom Gush Emunim puts on display, you may sometimes make the mistake of thinking that the differences between you are very small. Yoel Ben-Nun relates a conversation he had with Israeli writer Amos Oz, who supports the idea of a territorial compromise in the West Bank, and his conclusion in the wake of it was: "There is no chasm between us! There is no ideological conflict. The debate is only over the limits of the abilities of the Zionist enterprise today."

But the chasm exists.

It gaped, of course, when the Jewish underground was uncovered. But the underground was only a symptom. It gapes when I see in the house of moderate Yoel Ben-Nun a picture of the photomontage he made with Yehuda Etzion, leader of the underground: the Temple sitting on the Temple Mount (and Yoel Ben-Nun condemned the underground and castigated Etzion—and as a result lost standing in the movement).

And it gapes when Yoel Ben-Nun tells me that, in his eyes, we are not yet in Greater Israel—because the Jordan River is not the border of Greater Israel, but flows down its center. While he does not expect us to achieve that in this generation, he certainly feels obligated by the Bashan and the Gilad, once parts of Biblical Israel and now in Jordan.

Such talk frightens me. Once, the talk and writing about Jews returning to Beit-El and Hebron—such as the writings of Shabbatai Ben-Dov, who called in 1953 to strive for "the full messianic definition of the Israeli kingdom"—seemed daydreams disconnected from reality. Since then we have all learned, the hard way, that in Israel's special climate we must give serious attention to the visions of such people and their supporters. They, after all, see the Bible as an operational order. An operation that, even if its time is yet to come, will come and, if it does not come soon enough, will need to be brought. I fear life among people who have an obligation to an absolute order. Absolute orders require, in the end, absolute deeds, and I, nebbish, am a partial, relative, imperfect man who prefers to make correctible mistakes rather than attain supernatural achievements.

Who are these people who claim that they are acting in my name and in the name of my future (and who actually influence it decisively against my will), who are able to harden their hearts so much against others and against themselves, over the course of an entire generation or two, and become the kindling of the historical process they desire? What do I have to do with them? If they succeed in getting what they want, and if the opportunity presents itself (and in the inconstant Middle East it will eventually do so), and if they could proceed immediately to the next stage of realizing their grand plan, they will then be even stronger and more determined, wonderfully trained in hardening their hearts.

Who are these people who hurl themselves forward with spiritual devotion like a stone thrown from here into the clouds of the future and the promise, and all during their flight they are stone and solidity, splitting the air with power and determination, and when they finally hit ground, on a mountain or hill, they turn suddenly into a house of soft candlelight and the "warm Jewish heart"?

Who are these people who are able to pilot their lives with logic and clearheadedness into the very heart of a doubtful reality and then, upon arriving at a barrier which seems to all others impassable, metamorphose themselves into some other realm of existence, execute a sort of instant takeoff with the help of an Uzi, crossing the Messiah with a vertically launched aircraft, enter into an apocalyptic trance, dance like kids on the hilltops, shout ecstatic and ridiculous prophecies, and so, with determined blindness, with elimination of the self in order to allow the "together" to fill the soul, they are carried skyward, to the next target, and to the one after it, and wake up in the end with dawn on another hilltop, or in the heart of Hebron, red-eyed and battered by their drunken senses, fluttering toward us like spoiled children, and afterwards in provocation, and in the end in impudence and insolence?

I am too small to understand it.

Two weeks later, in the settlement Alfei Menashe, I heard Rav Levinger, the leader of the Jewish settlers in Hebron, say: "Fifty years ago our opponents argued

about Jaffa; today they argue with us about Alfei Menashe; in another fifty years they will argue with us about
Amman. That's the way it is."

I do not comprehend people who set history in motion.
The impresarios of history are beyond my understanding. They amuse themselves, I feel, with overly large toys,
and the game may come down on all our heads. For
instance, the game called "Blow Up the Dome of the
Rock and Wait One Turn for the Arab World's Reaction." Historical games often end in historical mistakes.

There will be a second underground. A second and a
third and a fourth. Just writing the words sickens me,
but it has to be said expressly: it will happen. They will
happen. Not from among the generation who gave birth
to the first Jewish underground—it was dealt a mortal
blow and is greatly broken, not necessarily because of
the deeds, but because a cruel mirror was placed in front
of its face. The first underground was not an accident
of history. It was the inevitable result of reality. So the
second one will be. I have noted elsewhere that the major
educational problem in Ofra is the lack of discipline
among the children, and that one of the women there
suggested that this is linked to the lawbreaking of Gush
Emunim.

In all that touches on the underground, the children
of Gush Emunim receive double messages from their
parents. It is enough to spend one evening with a family
in Ofra to realize this. Even the most prosaic of them
can evoke sudden wonder with their verbal acrobatics.
The bottom line of all this twisting and turning is this:
there is no regret. "We oppose the murder of the two
students at the Islamic college," the Granit parents say,
"but no one regrets the attack on the Arab mayors."

And the children—five and ten years old—listen, and are meant, it seems, to patch together some sort of philosophy and system of moral values in which one attempted murder is acceptable and another is not.

Would it be too much to believe that the leader of the Jewish underground of the 1990s is now studying in one of the yeshivas? The climate of the national religious public creates a sort of internal hierarchy, headed by those who are more committed than others to the absolute order. The mental steamroller which created characters like underground members Novick, Segel, and company has not stopped working. From the do-nothing clubbiness of what they lovingly and in awe call "our circles" will emerge now and in the future the hard and dim seed of absolute commitment. The mixed reaction they heard to the deeds of the underground from within Gush Emunim, as well as the indulgent attitude of some national leaders, was well understood by the potential terrorists now rocking over their books.

It is difficult for me to connect the pleasant people I met in Ofra with the obliquity of those who chant the words of the prophet Isaiah, "Take counsel together and it shall come to naught," but they are the same people. It is hard for me to understand Avital, who spoke with pain of the sufferings of Israeli Arabs, on whom we have forced Israeli citizenship, saying, "And I can justify every one of them who joins the PLO," but cannot feel the same emotion with regard to the Arabs of next-door Ain Yabrud, to whom she herself is a thorn in the side; it is difficult for me to grasp the declarations that "we hire no Arab laborers," but when I ask who built their houses, Shalmai, a sensitive and wise man, answers, "I don't know, little dwarves came one night and built them."

And these are the same people. I saw them in their calm days. Almost in their slack days. Not in the season of their messianic heat. Not at a time of "high messianic tension," but it lies in wait for them always, like a disease. These are historical people, and historical people become—at certain moments—hollow and allow history to stuff them, and then they are dangerous and deadly.

Until this is fully understood, we will all continue, gone foolish from abundance and apathy and feeling inferior in the face of "activism" and "realization of ideals," to sit in the hall and watch the *gushnikim* playing before us scenes of horror—at every opportunity that presents itself—yet stimulating some pleasant impulse in some hearts, as well as dramas of authentic pioneer idealism, and snatches of scenes of madness and instigation, except that sometimes, while we watch the events in that circular field and pay the small price of not doing anything, someone will awaken in the back corner of the great auditorium and will discover, when he sees the ground moving slowly under his feet, that this wonderful circus is a traveling one, traveling with determination, and that its goal and direction are known to him without any doubt.

5

Life Sciences

I told a friend of mine that I wanted to visit some classes at one of the West Bank universities. He said: "Classes? They go to classes there?" and laughed in amazement. "It never occurred to me that they go to classes. All we hear about them is that they throw stones and burn tires."

The doors on the classrooms at Bethlehem University have small glass windows. A stranger can peek through them and see the lesson in progress: the teacher, the pupils, and mostly the attentiveness. That is the first impression: the forward tilt—unconscious—of their bodies. The students hang on the teacher's every word. I have a green notebook in which I write as I listen to people, as I stand and as I walk. A long day of studies awaits me today.

In the hallway, near the stairwell, stand a lecturer and his students, conferring together. They speak about Freud. Humor as a way of expressing aggression, she says. I did my master's thesis on humor, he says. I also once took an entire course on humor, I remember, at the Hebrew University. We studied Freud and I wrote a long paper; I laugh quietly, to myself, like someone making a toast to another.

Hanging on the wall of the hallway is a very large bronze plaque depicting a lion cruelly overpowering a doe. Sitting under this familiar Palestinian symbol, on two chairs pulled together, are a boy and a girl. They whisper between them, her hair almost falling into his face. Ask people here about the role of politics in academic life, I note down to myself, and ask about permissiveness.

On the basement floor, the physics-department faculty lounge. Three professors take counsel with each other. Professor Zurub Abd-Al-Rahman explains their problem to me: the summer session generally runs six weeks, but because of the frequent closing of the university by the army, they have to make do with only four weeks of studies.

They refer to the calendar again and again, shaking their heads at each other with concern. We may need to give up on Electromagnetism B, one says.

The students won't be able to grasp the material, another says, making question marks next to the courses in danger of being canceled.

The third, an American professor working here on a Fulbright grant, tells me: "We can offer only the basic courses, the ones most necessary for their degree. Nothing else that can really enrich them, or expand their horizons."

Bethlehem University is fourteen years old. It was established by decree of the Vatican and has its backing.

About 1,500 students study at the university; the faculty numbers about 130. The West Bank has five accredited degree-granting universities. They enroll about ten thousand students. The largest of them is Bir Zeit, at this writing shut down for four months by order of the military administration, in the wake of violent demonstrations there. A few thousand more Arabs study at teachers' colleges, religious seminaries, technical schools, and commercial colleges. Bethlehem University is considered no less extreme in its politics than more-well-known Bir Zeit, and is known to be a stronghold of the Democratic Front for the Liberation of Palestine, a Marxist Palestinian faction. But because of the Vatican's support for the institution, the administration treats it with a bit more delicacy than it does the other West Bank universities.

Professor Hana Halaq suggests that I come with him to see the laboratories.

"When were you last closed?"

"We opened just yesterday, after three days of closure imposed in honor of your Independence Day. Here, this is our laboratory. Modest, I know. We make most of the equipment with our own hands. In the carpentry and metal shops."

Poor and primitive equipment. Microscopes and measuring instruments and Bunsen burners, all ancient-looking. A demonstration for students was in progress, and I had a quick lesson in the refraction of light. To the extent I could judge, the explanation was on the level of an Israeli high school. But more impressive was how the students related to the material—with respect and interest. Their expressions were totally concentrated.

Could I sit in on a class session?

Caught off guard, Hana Halaq removes his glasses and polishes them.

Not at all?

He avoids my gaze.

"Are there things you prefer to hide?"

"It is not a simple matter to let an Israeli into a class session. It would cause some tension."

"You mean that the students would be suspicious of a teacher who brought an Israeli to class? Even to a mathematics lesson?"

"Let's continue our tour. I will show you our greenhouse."

"Do you have courses in politics and current events here?"

"Take a look at the catalogue."

The catalogue is attractive and written in English. On the cover is a photograph of the university's stone quarters—the carved steeple with the statue of the Madonna above, and a large clock with its hands pointing to five minutes after twelve.

Course 201—Political Science 1. This course deals with the following subjects: social environment, the society's metamorphosis into a political entity, types of sovereignty . . .

Course 304—The Palestinian Problem. Detailed study of the problem, focusing on decisive events. Historical documents, people and organizations involved in the situation. Object of the course: to clarify the problem, in an effort to understand it in perspective.

But there is also Course 311—Drama. Critical study of the development of the drama as a literary genre.

There will be an emphasis on the influence of the classical and European theater on dramatic works in the English language . . .

Course 431—The Exceptional Child. Through comparison with the normal child, the course will survey the gifted, the creative, the retarded, the blind, and the socially inhibited child . . . There will be an emphasis on personal and social problems and on modern methods of treating them.

And this, too: Course 438—Israeli Society. This course is aimed at acquainting the student with Israeli society, and how its melting pot brought together groups so different and heterogeneous in their customs, traditions, and cultures, and made them into one homogeneous society composed of subgroups.

Hana Halaq leads me to the almost-empty greenhouse. A few shrunken cactuses and geranium plants. Biology students learn plant anatomy from these plants. From the greenhouse in which I stand I gaze outward, toward the wonderfully beautiful campus lawn—flower boxes, stone buildings, stately pine trees, gravel paths. Hundreds of students and they make hardly any noise. Most of them are sitting, during their break, in the sunlight, studying alone or in groups. It reminds one, slightly, of the pictures of Plato's school in Athens.

I absorb their seriousness, penetrating even the glass walls of the greenhouse. Hard work is in the air of this small campus, an atmosphere of study. Whoever says that the universities are hothouses of terror does not understand the complexity of the issue. There is something deeper and more fundamental here. I wrote the following in my notebook: "There is no idleness. Not like the campus quadrangles I know. Here they seem, somehow, determined. Even during their breaks."

Back to the bustling corridor. It is very crowded. A new, elegant wing of the university has just been completed, but the military administration approved it on condition that it not contain a single classroom—only a restaurant and administrative offices. It will not solve the overcrowding. Here, over the large stones of the floor, someone guides a wheelchair: the body and face of a small boy. Maybe a young genius. His chin droops on his chest. Thick glasses over his eyes. Everyone races between the classrooms. The space is full of youth and chatter. Boys and girls exchange glances. By the way, there are as many women studying here as men, and the teachers say the women are the best students: first, because the most talented men find their way to other countries, and a girl, as talented as she might be, will not go far from her father's house; second, because they are less involved in politics. I note that almost all the students are well dressed. None is sloppy. You can feel that people come here with respect, almost in celebration. I try to guess at the backgrounds of those passing by me. Who is the son of the rich man, whose father and grandfather are educated and learned and sent the young man to continue the family tradition, and who is the son of the poor fellah, peasant, who only reluctantly gave up his son's labor because the boy insisted on continuing his education and pleaded that the father allow him to change his life, because the neighbors said that the boy has the head of a government minister, because even if the family eats less bread during these years, the father himself feels that in making his son a student he is rebelling against the fate which is strangling him.

From among the milling crowd I make out a crown of red hair. The face of a young boy. Striding in the middle of a knot of students. This redhead from Bethlehem jokes non-stop, eager to entertain. I join them in their walk to class, look for the girl he is trying to impress, and think I have found her. I don't think he'll succeed.

Two short conversations:

Professor James Connolly, chairman of the English department: "I am here because it is an important service to the population. The students here are eager to learn. They are never satiated by their studies. In many ways I prefer them to those in England. Their motivation to gain knowledge is immense. Of course, the general level here is lower than in a Western university. We try to admit as many students as possible. There are difficult entrance examinations, but we accept mediocre students as well. We have to meet a great demand."

"What do you teach here?"

"I teach English poetry. They are so sensitive to lyric rhythm! Maybe because the rhythm of the Koran flows in their blood."

"What will you be teaching in your next class?"

"The poetry of John Donne."

"How do they relate to his wild sensuality?"

"At first they are very confused. Then they are conquered."

"And does what is called 'the situation' make its way into the class?"

"I try to prevent it. My status here as a foreign lecturer is very sensitive. Other teachers have been expelled from the West Bank after being accused of incitement. Sometimes, in English-language classes, I ask them to write a composition on what concerns them. Then I get not a few compositions on their suffering under the occupation."

"And what do you do in such cases?"

He throws me a blue-eyed, British, sly smile: "Why, I correct the mistakes in the English, of course."

Muhammad Haj Yihia teaches social work. He is a native of Teibe, an Israeli Arab village, and a graduate of the Hebrew University of Jerusalem.

"The first year here is hard for every student. Don't forget that they generally come from a traditional society, that they are the products of an unadvanced public-school curriculum, and that they have for the most part studied only with others of their own sex. All this affects the students' spirit and intellectual ability. They are not an open people. They are used to learning by rote, memorization, to having to guess at the desire of the authoritative teacher. At first they are incapable of working on their own and thinking as individuals. They lack even the tools needed to develop self-awareness.

"I, as a teacher, endeavor to pass on to my students the approach I learned at the Hebrew University: independence, critical thinking, and curiosity. I tell them not to base themselves on a single source of information, that they not accept anything I say as dogma, that they should always question. At first, they actually get angry at me: they do not succeed in overcoming the obstacles within them. Afterwards, they do overcome them and break loose. This is the most important education I can give them. I could have found work at the Hebrew University, but there I would have been only a lecturer in social work. Here I am also an educator. That is a big difference."

A loudspeaker suddenly barks outside. From the window I see a student in a black leather jacket gathering people around him. Students from every corner of the courtyard come to listen to him. He voices a furious protest against the university cafeteria serving food today, at the height of Ramadan, the Moslem holy month of fasting. "Oh, it's only a demonstration of fanatical Moslems," says a Christian student working in the room, but those around me exchange quick glances.

As the demonstration continues, I talk with a student with an official position in the student government, who refuses to give me his name and who dictates a stream of tired and insincere declarations. He finds it necessary to raise his voice in order to be heard over the noise of the demonstration outside. The shouts coming from the demonstration now turn into the regular chants of a chorus. I get up to look and see that the pastoral courtyard already contains hundreds of students, gathered in tight circles around the speaker. He shouts a phrase, and they answer him with a roar, waving their fists in the air. To my surprise, they are now crying hostile anti-Israel and anti-occupation slogans. The object of their anger has switched so quickly. In the crowd are many white-kerchiefed women. They are the most extreme of the female Moslems who study here. Someone pulls me gently away from the window. Better that they not know I am here. Bring that man out to us, like Lot in Sodom. But even a stolen glance allows me to make out that

redhead among the sea of darker ones. Now he is completely foreign, waving his fist with the others and thun-
dering with all his might. Oddly, that is the main thing
that remains in my memory from this moment—being
totally disappointed with a person whom I did not even
know.

One of those present in the room walks away from
the window, looks at me, and says in a swallowed voice:
"We have a little problem outside." I examine the en-
ergetically moving lips of the official student, flower of
the politicians, dictating to me his tired text, in which
the sentences could easily be switched around without
any damage to its actual intention, and as he speaks I
write the following in my green notebook: Now, the
truth. Are you afraid? Yes. And if something happens
to you here, if they hurt you, do you think it will cause
you to revise your opinions? To begin to surrender to
hate? And if they were to hurt your child?

I set down the answer for the record and as personal
testimony, and it is all written there, in the green notebook.

The campus calms down within half an hour, and I
emerge into the courtyard. I present myself to a group
of students and ask to talk with them. They giggle awk-
wardly and suddenly look very young. One of them takes
up the challenge and rises. I am willing to talk, but not
here. Her name is Raula, from Ramallah, and she is
studying social work. "I wanted a profession that would
allow me to give something to people. Something that
would give me an opportunity to work with my heart
and not just with my head or hands." She leads me
through the bustling courtyard, through the piercing

glances, to a room that looks like the office of some sort of cultural committee: metal cabinets overflowing with posters, tables piled with pamphlets, stacks of newspapers. A red-tinted map of Palestine is stuck on a wooden board, with the caption "Palestine Is Ours." On one wall is a picture of Che Guevera, and on another a drawing of a long-haired girl, with strong brown eyes. "Her name is Taghrid Batma," Raula tells me, as her voice takes on a special color, as if she is telling a folktale. "Israeli intelligence agents killed her in '82. Why? Because she was a good Palestinian. She organized many demonstrations and was an activist. That's why."

For some reason I do not feel like speaking to her about the side the Palestinians present to us, the Israelis, and I ask about the couple I saw whispering to each other in the corridor, about the glances exchanged between boys and girls in the courtyard, about that hardly hidden fluttering of eyes that makes the atmosphere of this campus more charged and potent than at Israeli universities. Raula laughs for a minute. "Relations between men and women here are very free. Why are you surprised? We are educated, progressive adults, and we know what to do with the culture we have acquired."

"Did your parents agree that you live this way, so close together with men?"

"My mother knew exactly what happens here, and she sent me here anyway. Besides, we all know that the university is the greatest matchmaker for educated young people, so maybe Mother was thinking of that, too."

"And does the situation allow you to study as well, or are your minds distracted by other things?"

"The occupation weighs down on us here. We never know if there will be classes tomorrow, or if they will allow us past the roadblocks on the way to the university. In class we are afraid to express our opinions freely, because we are afraid of spies. You know, two years ago they caught some collaborators here. They beat them and expelled them from here. Afterwards, some of them were found dead, and they never discovered who killed them. There is always tension in class, because everything is connected in one way or another to the situation. We really live under pressure, but that is what creates the motivation to keep at our studies and to continue with our daily lives. It is a pioneer challenge, because with all the disturbances and closures and pressures we still exist and study like in any other university in the world, and we do our best to get through all the material. That's an iron rule with us, with the teachers and the students, a rule we accepted of our own volition: we make up all the required material, no matter what happens, even if it means classes in the evening, during vacations, at people's houses. Here every class lasts at least an hour and a quarter, not forty-five minutes as at your university. We aren't lazy. We have a goal, you know." Her small mouth forms a determined circle. "We must educate ourselves, in opposition to what the occupation wants us to be. The occupation can numb, and we must fight that numbness. That is our mission. There are those among us who fight with weapons, and there are those who fight with speeches. We will fight with the help of education and thought."

6

The Yellow Wind

And there are also refugees for whom a miracle happened and who were returned to their land.

Such an instance, of incomprehensible mercy, is that of those who reside in the village in Wadi Alfuqin: in 1948 they were uprooted from their village, and for twenty-four years they lived in a refugee camp, or with family members who took pity on them, or in rented houses, the houses of strangers, in Jericho and Deheisha and Husan and Amman, and suddenly, in 1972, some remote emperor lifted his little finger and gave the order: "Return them!" and they returned to the village from which they were exiled, and they, perhaps, are the only ones to have returned from refugee life to that of human beings, and they can testify to the differences, and can say something about the chances for reconciliation and forgiveness. I went there.

Wadi Alfuqin is a fertile, watered valley. Springs flow, the ground is productive and benevolent, and everyone has a storage pool for springwater, and kitchen gardens full of produce, and olive groves bordered by grapevines planted shoulder to shoulder. And at the top of the mountain which stands over the valley are the foundations of the ancient city of Beitar, and the new settlement Beitar Elit.

After the War of Independence, the valley was the focus of attacks on Israeli Army patrols passing nearby, along the border, and after the army took several retaliatory actions, the village was abandoned and its natives dispersed. Nearly all the houses in the village were demolished, and the ruins on the mountain slope are still bleached by the sun, and the remaining houses have become a training site for the army. On some of the ruins one can still make out the marks of the bullets fired by soldiers in the fifties.

Imtiyaz (the name means "excellence") had not yet been born when her parents fled from the village. They moved from place to place in the West Bank over the course of several years. When she was a baby, they came to the Deheisha refugee camp. She lived her entire childhood and youth in the camp, and a year ago she returned to Wadi Alfuqin: she married a man there. Her parents, who could not afford to build a house in the village, remained in Deheisha. She remembers the day, fifteen years ago, when the people of Alfuqin left the refugee camp and returned to their village. "Of course we were mad at them," she says. "We were angry that they were returning here to real life, and we remained there, in prison. They cried with happiness, and we cried out of jealousy and pain. There are still some there today who are angry with those who were able to return."

"They are mad at the ones who returned? What are they guilty of?"

"Whom should they be angry at?"

Whom, indeed? "The Jews threw us out of here, and the Jews brought us back." A wide-eyed old woman sighs as she listens to us from the roof of the house next door, between clumps of just-sheared sheep's wool hung out for air: the Jew taketh away and the Jew giveth.

It is a cool day in early spring. We are sheltered in a shady, broad yard, and the little valley lies at our feet, and the storage pools sparkle in the sun, and despite the Ramadan fast, my hosts bring me a glass of tea, and little by little people from every corner of the village gather around us, listening, nodding their heads, and telling their stories—but not freely. These are things people do not like to recall.

"Life in the camp is bad," one woman of about fifty says shyly. "You are always with your head down, waiting for the next blow. After a few years there you have nothing left but fear and poverty. You become like a dead person: you do not want anything and you do not hope. You wait for death. Even the children there are old. They are born with fear. Here, children are like children: they almost do not know what the army is. Only the *mustawtanin*, the settlers, are frightening."

Everyone glances upward, to the bauble of a settlement stuck into the mountain.

"When the families left Deheisha on their way back to the village and we stayed there," Imtiyaz relates, "I cried for nearly a week. They can return and we can't, because we didn't have the money to build a new house. I was small, and I didn't understand that. After all, we all lived like one big family, we shared everything, we suffered together for years, so why them and not us? After a while, when they began to come visit us in the camp, we would pelt them with questions. We wanted to know everything about the village: how the land was and the spring and the vegetables . . ."

"They would bring us vegetables in bags," remembers Hanan, a rounded young woman who knows a few words of Hebrew. "And we would kiss those vegetables. We would kiss each tomato a hundred times before we ate it there."

"But I actually like Deheisha and miss it," a woman says hotly. She has strong features and had come to sit across from me on a stool, her legs held apart, and had immediately begun vilifying our hosts for serving me a drink during Ramadan. "Even if your brother comes," she says to the taken-aback woman of the house, "do not give him anything to drink! Ah, when the Jordanians were here, they would shoot anyone who desecrated the fast. Since you came here, everything has changed. There is no respect for religion anymore."

You miss Deheisha?

Even the retarded woman, kneeling by the wall and hollowing out green squashes to be stuffed with rice and meat, stops to make a circular motion with her hand and looks at her in amazement.

"Yes. I miss it. I get goose bumps when I think of it," she says, and bares an arm to illustrate her meaning. "But there it's bad! Frightening!" Imtiyaz counters her, and she responds: "The fear is their doing"—indicating me with a movement of her head. "And I miss the people who were there. I miss my house. What, aren't they people, the ones there? Weren't we close to them? That's what I miss."

Apparently she is right, I think. A person can miss even a hard, bad place, if there were beautiful moments there, and if he has a memory of a single instance of grace, and maybe loved someone there or was loved. I thought of the army bases in the Sinai where I once served, jumbles of iron and cement thrown at random on a mountain, and how we made our lives there full, and how those neutral, dead places became dear to us.

Another woman joins the group, greeting us and sitting by us, and another young man, who brings us mandrake fruit to smell. Here it is called the "madman's apple," and it has a faint and wonderful aroma.

The name of the woman who just arrived is Wadha Isma'il, and she listens for a while to the stories of the others. Afterwards, she begins to speak, in a moderate tone, without any reproach in her voice, and tells me this: "After they expelled us from the village, we would come back to work our land. The Israeli Army pretended not to see us. They would have maneuvers up on the mountain, and we would work the land in the valley. We would come every day by donkey from Hebron in order to work our land. One day I came here with my father. I was young then, almost a girl. We worked a few hours, and we started on our way back home. Suddenly the Israeli soldiers surrounded us and separated me from my father. I saw that they blindfolded him with a rag and pushed him into some bushes. I remember that he still had a chance to turn to me once and call to me through the rag. Immediately afterwards I heard shots. Many shots. I began to cry. The soldiers who had stayed with me asked me: Who is that man to you? I said: He is my father. They said: Go to the garden down there, and you'll see that he is harvesting lettuce and eggplant. When I was some distance from them, I glanced back and I saw one of the soldiers aiming his rifle at me. I was frightened and bent over. His bullet hit my neck and came out on the other side."

I don't know what to say to her, and she interprets my silence, apparently, as disbelief. "Look," she says, and her work-hardened fingers undo her kerchief, and she smiles a sort of apology about having to bother me with her wound. I see an ugly scar in back, and another ugly scar in front. Young Hanan cries. It seems that Wadha is her mother. "Every time I hear that story, it is as if it were the first time," Hanan says.

Wadha lay among the bushes and played dead. The soldiers distanced themselves from her and then left the area. She rose, oozing blood, and bound her wounds with a handkerchief. Afterwards, she found her father on the ground, his hands tied behind his back, a large rock on his neck. There were thirty bullets in his body, the village elder, Abu Harb, told us later. Wadha, who is for a moment a girl once more, describes with movements of her body how she walked and tripped through the valley, at night, scared that the Israelis would shoot her from behind, or the Jordanians from in front. She concluded her story as she began it, quietly, with no tone of accusation, and her daughter Hanan stood and cried for all of us.

I pondered then about how much one must be suspicious of people who testify about themselves morning and night that they are merciful. They always taught us that we do not know how to be cruel or to hate our enemies, really hate. We are cleanhanded types. And despite that, every so often another ugly incident takes place, carried out by the merciful hands of people like us, people who never hate, and maybe the fact that we do not allow ourselves to hate actually testifies to the disparagement we feel toward the Arabs, since you do not hate a person whom you see as lower than you. It is hard for us, for instance, to hate children, because we sense that they are not our equals. In this context I recalled a story told me by a reserve soldier I met during the course of these seven weeks. It has no connection with Wadi Alfuqin, but it is very much connected to the entire matter.

"Once, when I was on reserve duty, there was a terrorist attack in the Old City in Jerusalem, near the Rockefeller Museum, and we set up a detainment area for Arab suspects in the courtyard of police headquarters. We picked up all the Arabs we caught. We brought entire truckloads. How I beat them that night! There was another reservist, a young guy, with me, and I saw that every Arab he catches, he bites hard on the ear. Actually takes off a piece. I ask him why he did it, and he answered me: 'So that I'll know them next time we meet.' "

At the top of the village, in a small, dark house, next to the house of his extended family, the village elder lives. He is called Abu Harb, and he is eighty-five years old. He is, according to the residents, the village historian.

He sits on a colored reed mat, his shaking hand playing with a large, antiquated transistor radio. His eyes are much swollen, and his nose is oddly reddish. He remembers the Turks and the English and the Egyptians, who were here briefly, and the Jordanians he remembers, and now us. "In October 1948 we were exiled from here," he says (the only one in the village, he says, who knows the precise date), and for twenty-four years we were not here. We wandered from place to place for twenty-four years, and everywhere we went we would bury our dead, and afterwards we would wander onward, and for twenty-four years I did not sleep at night, I would lie awake and think, and the first night I returned to my village and slept in it was the happiest night of my life, because I slept on my own land."

In 1972 the people of the village received a notice from the military government that they could return to their village. They do not know who made the decision. They received a notice, and that same day the news spread to all the village's exiles, who had been dispersed to the four winds. When Abu Harb describes how they gathered and came here, I recall the book of Ezekiel, the vision of the dry bones which join together, cover themselves with flesh and sinew, and return to life.

"The military government gave us one month to return to the village," Abu Harb relates. "They told us that whoever did not build a house within that month would not be allowed to return. We came that same night, from every place, and we set up booths and tents in the place that was once the village. Afterwards, we collected money and paved an asphalt road to bring construction materials in trucks. It was a harsh summer and we worked day and night, and we would sleep under the floor of the house we were building. Each one of us built a single room with a roof, and that was our claim."

He tells his story, and his wife, Ratiba, enters the room. She looks younger than he and her face is still smooth. Her face is dark, "but that is not my color from birth, it is only because of the damned sun of the camp, in Jericho," she explains. They have been married for sixty years, "and he never took another wife, other than me!" she boasts.

I asked them if they know why the Israeli authorities so suddenly allowed them to return to their village.

"We heard that the Israelis needed our place in Deheisha. They intended to bring to the camp a large group of Gazans whom they wanted to remove from the Gaza Strip. So they evacuated us."

"And did Gazans actually take your place there?"

"They came. But afterwards they stopped transferring people there from Gaza."

I do not know if that is the correct interpretation of this singular act of mercy. The fact is that it was all done in secrecy, under wraps. Maybe so as not to arouse demands from other exiles in the territories, or from Israeli Arabs who had been expelled from their villages. I tend to think that the explanation given by the people of Wadi Alfuqin, concerning their exchange for Gazans, is correct. In the twisted climate of the occupation, when one act of mercy is performed, it must almost of necessity be crooked and bent, and be nothing but another of the many faces of arbitrariness.

I ask my conversants how the return to their land affected them.

"Everything changed," Abu Harb says. "We now live here among real people. The people who stayed behind in Deheisha and in Jericho are miserable. They are going mad from sadness and longing for their land. They come and plead with us to give them a little garden plot. Just so they can regain a little self-respect. Something to live for. After all, it is not just land, it is everything. They are cut off from everything there. They have ceased to be people. We have been planted anew. Not only in the land. The land is the beginning: we are planted in life as a whole. In normal relations with other people. In tradition. In all the right things. We are no longer strangers in the world. We have the milk of our cows, the flour of our wheat. We are now complete people."

I have one more question. Maybe the most important question: The Israelis brought you back to your village. Do you hate them less now?

They exchange glances. The very old man, his wife, his daughter-in-law, his many grandchildren and great-grandchildren, all of whom have gathered in the room. The daughter-in-law speaks. She relates that her husband has been arrested on suspicion of taking part in terrorist acts. Immediately after his arrest, Israeli soldiers came and destroyed their house. It was a new house, just completed. The family was not given enough time to remove all its belongings. When it was destroyed, it collapsed on ten sacks of sugar and ten sacks of flour that had been bought at great cost and had been stored in the house for the housewarming celebration. The husband was released right afterwards without any charges having been brought against him. As she tells the story, her lips go white with fury and look like a whip scar on her face. Two other sons of Abu Harb are now under arrest in Israel. One is in prison and the other is awaiting trial. Abu Harb says: Both of them are innocent. And if they did something, they apparently had no choice. The injustice and bad effects of the situation are what turns normal people into criminals.

The mother, Ratiba, says: "The settlers come down

from the mountain at night with dogs. They frighten us. They stole our spring, and call it sharing."

"The bus that takes their children to school," ten-year-old grandson Hazem says, "blocks the way for our bus every day, and we have to walk about a kilometer to school."

"They will expel us from here again," says another young man, about eighteen, and everyone nods in agreement.

"And then we will really go mad," says Grandmother Ratiba.

The old man, Abu Harb, sighs a long sigh, passes his hand over his face, and presses it against his eyes. The small children watch him. Returning home did not turn the heart of any one of them into one which loves us, the Israelis. Maybe it was foolish even to hope for that. Abu Harb rises to his feet with difficulty, and sees me to the door. We stand and look together over the beautiful and peaceful valley, and the smoke from the straw fires curls up into the air, and the thistles and wildflowers bloom as far as one can see. Now is the time of the yellow flowers. I tell Abu Harb that I called my book *The Yellow Time* in Hebrew, and he asks me if I have heard about the yellow wind. I say that I haven't, so he begins telling me about it, and about the yellow wind that will soon come, maybe even in his lifetime: the wind will come from the gate of Hell (from the gates of Paradise comes only a pleasant, cool wind)—*rih asfar*, it is called by the local Arabs, a hot and terrible east wind which comes once in a few generations, sets the world afire, and people seek shelter from its heat in the caves and caverns, but even there it finds those it seeks, those who have performed cruel and unjust deeds, and there, in the cracks in the boulders, it exterminates them, one by one. After that day, Abu Harb says, the land will be covered with bodies. The rocks will be white from the heat, and the mountains will crumble into a powder which will cover the land like yellow cotton.

7

Catch-44

The military court in Nablus. An ugly, dirty, dark building. As soon as I was inside I felt a need to contract, make myself small, to keep from touching other objects; the windows are broken and filthy. Through the spiderwebs one can make out the silhouette of barren Mt. Ibal, the mountain of the curses. Outside, storms frequently cut off the electricity, and in the dark it is sometimes hard to see the justice being done here. I enter the courtroom in the middle of a trial. The accused—a skinny boy with a scarred face—is charged with membership in an enemy organization. The defense attorney summarizes his arguments. He recalls that the boy merely expressed interest in joining the Fatah, and did not actually become a member, and furthermore, he is sick, his knees jut forward, from birth, your honor, stand up for a minute so they can see, here, and his father is over there, your honor, he would like to say something, he promises to be responsible for the behavior of the boy in the future, there's no time, your honor? So if the father can only stand up, so you can see what kind of person he is.

From among the public benches the father rises. A man of about fifty, short, with a wrinkle-lined face. He crumples his hat in his hands. Takes a hesitant step forward, and slowly, slowly, raises his eyes to the judge, as if laying out before him a complex and delicate exhibit for the trial, and actually, his face is all he has to exhibit in his defense: his son's guilt is absolutely clear. A stupid and simple boy, the father's face says, perhaps your honor also has young children and he knows how it is with them, the face murmurs, and I can see that even the judge has been caught up in the fear of that expression.

He may be seated.

He sits down beside his overgrown wife, thick of limb, whose lips mutter unceasingly. The rest of the family look frozen at the judge, hanging on his words. The father's face calms little by little.

The military judge, Major Yair Rabinowitz (himself once a military prosecutor), sentences the accused to four months in prison, with a one-year suspended sentence in force for three years. The defendant goes to prison, throws a smile of relief at his brothers, not at his parents. He is surprised at the leniency of the punishment. The mother looks at the father in agitation and bites her lips: four months!

Next case.

When lawyer Leah Tsemel arrives at the parking lot opposite the military court in Nablus, her clients pounce on her car, besiege her in fear and supplication, thirsty for the news she brings. In her office in East Jerusalem, in a broken house with a shattered roof, Arabs whose actions have brought them, or members of their families, up against the Israeli judicial system wait for her from the early morning, confused and ignorant of their rights and obligations and what is going to happen to them. The office teems with people, mostly villagers, who sit there for hours, and who greet Tsemel with awe. She is a small woman, always smiling, resolute in her speech, most extreme in her opinions, sympathetic and honest. She conducts several conversations at once with all those massed around her, speaking with them in excellent Arabic with an unmistakable Jewish Ashkenazi accent, chain-smoking, arguing over the telephone with police investigators who are preventing her from seeing a client of hers in jail, curses, forgives, puts on glasses missing one sidepiece, sets out on her way, to Nablus or Ramallah. The high energy she exudes threatens any calmer beings close by with adrenaline poisoning. Something else ought to be noted: in her relations with Arabs there is something you don't come across very often—straightforwardness and equality, without a trace of sanctimony; she places herself neither above nor below her clients, and there is no soft and self-effacing paternalism. Very rare.

And now—the trial of Jafer Haj Hassan, accused of having made contact with an enemy organization.

He is different from the prisoners shut up in the small, filthy confinement room. He stands tall and has delicate features. His movements are moderate and quiet. The prosecutor explains the charge: a few years ago Hassan asked his father for a sum of money in order to study in Germany. His father applied to a friend of his, a Fatah member in Jordan, and asked for assistance. Jafer Haj Hassan did not receive money but did receive a scholarship to study German in Germany. After half a year's work, he decided that he did not want to study German and changed his field. His patron in the Fatah told his father that the organization would support him only if he pursued a subject of some benefit to the organization. He refused—and his scholarship was immediately revoked. Hassan remained in Germany several years, with no links to terrorist organizations, married a German woman, and then came home. A week later he was arrested. He has been in the Nablus prison for forty-four days. A security detainee.

Forty-four days. They did not beat him there, he tells me afterwards; the treatment was reasonable. Even so, he says, do you know what forty-four days in jail is? Previously, he had not been involved in politics at all. Did not even know what it meant to be a Palestinian. One may assume that in prison he learned something. Forty-four days. A trimester course in national consciousness.

The judge listens to the prosecutor's arguments. He wears a knitted *kipah* and has a pleasant face. He also has a businessman's black swivel chair, which may be moved in any direction, and which may be bent backward, rising and falling with ease. The prosecutor, a young officer in the standing army, enumerates the charges. The room is dim. Uniformity is congealed on the faces of the reserve soldiers guarding the courtroom, on the face of the prosecutor, the translator, the woman soldier-stenographer. Only the judge rocks back and forth on the raised platform. For a second, his head disappears entirely behind his desk. The court holds its breath. Then he sweeps up slowly, raising with him an interesting argument: from the charge, it would seem that the suspect never had real, active contact or connection of any sort with a terrorist organization. There was never any direct connection between them. He maintained—so to speak—contact with his father. What is wrong with that, the judge asks. After all, it was his father—who is now in Jordan—who had made the contact, etc.

The prosecutor, lacking a little experience, here makes a mistake and does not accept the hinted advice of the judge. He sticks to his arguments: the accused should have distinguished between those conversations with his father regarding family matters and those regarding terrorist organizations. The translator—a heavyset Druse soldier with no expression resident on his face—had some time ago ceased to translate the proceedings for the accused. He picks his ears with his finger, whispers something to the stenographer, and again sinks into a deep vegetative stupor, accompanied by additional unconscious bodily movements. The relatives of the accused gaze at him in supplication: he is their sole connection with what is being said, but he has become habituated to them and pays no attention. Only an angry admonition from the judge brings him back to life: he resumes translating for several minutes, and then, little by little, is reabsorbed into that addicting oblivion.

Defense attorney Tsemel rises from her seat and protests the use of the term "terrorist organization." The judge asks to hear the reason for her objection. Tsemel reminds him that British law calls it a "proscribed association."

The judge: But the term "terrorist organization" has been used here for years!

Tsemel: That's because of Mehahem Kornwitz, the

prosecutor who was from Gush Emunim. He changed the term at his own initiative, and suddenly all the charge sheets were filled with "terrorist organizations." So, inevitably, every accused person is a "terrorist," and that, of course, influences the judges in making their decisions.

The prosecutor (slightly mocking): And Madam, of course, has not come to terms with that distortion.

Tsemel: Correct. I have refused on principle to accept charge sheets in which the term "terrorist" is used. Judges have always conceded me the point, but I did not want only consideration.

The judge: So what did Madam do?

Tsemel: I applied to the chief counsel in the territories and asked that he instruct prosecutors not to use the term "terrorists" when drafting charges.

The judge (amused): And what, Madam, was the counsel's answer?

Tsemel: He said that I am right, but did nothing. For a year and a half I have been sending him requests. Just this week the corrective instruction arrived, and I demand that from now on it be adhered to with care.

The judge: As far as I'm concerned, it can be called a "charitable organization." The prosecutor will now continue to relate the accused's connections with the Salvation Army.

The accused understands neither the amused trialogue nor the reading of the charge sheet. No one explains to him what is being said. He is caught in an incomprehensible nightmare and does not know how it will end. His situation is, however, better than that of an ordinary defendant here, because most of them who arrive in the courtroom have already confessed their guilt at an early stage, while being interrogated by the security service. In 95 percent of the cases, the defense attorney is forced to satisfy himself with bargaining over the severity of the sentence, rather than over whether punishment should be imposed on his client in the first place.

Here, however, the charge sheet may be disproven easily. The judge is also aware of this, and he wavers out loud: Is maintaining contact with his father sufficient to convict the defendant?

The prosecution and defense finish their presentations. The judge withdraws to his chambers. The prosecutor, the defense attorney, and the translator wait for him in one of the secretarial offices of the court. The place is humming with young men and women soldiers, who while away their military service here. Several of them are currently sprawled on a pile of mattresses, chatting. The walls are decorated with cutouts from an Israeli teen magazine and with the same pseudo-clever posters which hang in every army office: "The Lazy Man's Ten Commandments," "Today Is the First Day of the Rest of Your Life." To think that they serve three years of life experience and routine here, organize going-away parties ("And from all of us success in civilian life, and don't forget us"), to think that here they fall in love.

"He has to free him," Leah Tsemel erupts. "It shouldn't be open to question. The matter is completely clear!" The prosecutor, young, blond, and bearded, smiles with a sort of strange wisdom, older than his years.

Both he and she know that the decisive majority of trials in the military courts in the area end in conviction. They both know that the defendant—if convicted—will not be able to appeal the judgment, because in the "territories" only a single level of courts functions, hearing every kind of case, without any appeals court above it. There is always tension between the civil jurists and the military people dealing with the law: the army, of course, prefers to see the court as part of the executive arm of the military. The regulations regarding the legal handling of prisoners reflect this: in the "territories," a suspect may be held prisoner without a court order for eighteen days (in Israel, no more than forty-eight hours); in Israel, the police must allow the defendant to meet his lawyer as soon as possible, within, at the most, forty-eight hours. Under the military government, the court responsible for the prison may delay the meeting between the prisoner and his lawyer for as long as it cares to.

The judge still wavers.

I recall the George Orwell essay "Shooting an Elephant." Orwell, while serving in the British Army in Burma, is drafted by a Burmese mob to kill a giant elephant in heat. As he strides toward the elephant— pressed by the expectations of the crowd—he first understands that he may not be as free to decide his own actions as he thought beforehand.

In his chambers, the judge delves into the case of Jafer Haj Hassan. Hundreds of thousands of inhabitants of the West Bank and Gaza have, as defendants or as relatives of defendants, passed through the military courts of Israel. They have waited in the mildewed corridors, have raised frightened and confused glances at the judge determining their fate and the fate of their families; have listened without comprehending to the defense and prosecuting attorneys bargaining in the hall over the severity of the punishment to be inflicted. There is not, it seems, any way to impose security and order in these areas without military courts, but there must be a way to make this massive friction between Israelis and Palestinians more honorable and tolerable, and minimize the hate as much as possible.

The judge still wavers.

Orwell says: "And suddenly I realized that I should have to shoot the elephant after all. The people expected it of me and I had got to do it; I could feel their two thousand wills pressing me forward, irresistibly. And it was at this moment, as I stood there with the rifle in my hands, that I first grasped the hollowness, the futility of the white man's dominion in the East. Here was I, the white man with his gun, standing in front of the unarmed native crowd—seemingly the leading actor of the piece; but in reality I was only an absurd puppet pushed to and fro by the will of those yellow faces behind."

The judge's chambers are still closed.

Because there is a catch.

Catch-44.

Since the defendant, Jafer Haj Hassan, had already spent forty-four days in prison, the judge faced a serious problem. Can a military court of an occupying power admit that the military government of the occupation made a mistake? And how will that influence its authority, esteem, and power in the eyes of the inhabitants?

Everything depends on the answer to this question.

Perhaps it is because of this question that the judge has been wrapped up in himself for two whole hours.

Here. He returns.

All rise!

The judgment: I sentence the defendant to forty-four days in prison. The crime: bringing money into the area in violation of section 2a-1.

The defense attorney does not believe her ears. Even the prosecutor smiles uncomfortably.

This requires a brief explanation. After two hours of uncertainty, the judge has decided to convict the defendant of a new charge not included in the original charge sheet! The law establishes that such a conviction ("a conviction without informing the defense counsel that the defendant is liable to be convicted on this charge, and without giving the defense counsel notice of intent to convict on this section") is directly contrary to section 23 of the order on security regulations. In a case in which the court revises the list of charges, it must (according to the same order) "allow the defense counsel to postpone the hearing or reexamine the witnesses, before the court may continue with its judgment."

None of these things was done here.

And note well: the accused did not bring money into the area. He received a scholarship. That is, a benefit. In Germany. And Germany is not in this area.

All rise!

Catch-44 is a combination of two Catch-22s.

One of them says something like this: If his honor the judge acquits the defendant on all charges, the inhabitants of the "territories" may interpret this as weakness. His acquittal is liable to call into question the sensitive system of relations between the inhabitants and the government authority, and riots, demonstrations, and so on may break out. General and personal security will be put in danger, and the defendant himself is liable to find himself in prison in the wake of a general escalation of tension, which may sweep him along with it. So that if he is acquitted, he is liable to be arrested.

The other catch is this: If his honor the judge imposes

a punishment of forty-four-day imprisonment on the accused, the inhabitants will understand immediately that the occupying power cannot allow itself to appear in error even in an unimportant case like this one, and this implies a great and dangerous weakness, which may, God forbid, endanger the sensitive system of relations ... riots ... arrests ... and the accused will find himself again behind bars.

In this light, the retroactive sentence of Jafer Haj Hassan to forty-four days in prison should be seen as a preemptive acquittal.

The defendant is freed immediately. The judge disappeared even before that. The black, authoritative chair still rocks up and down in a suspicious way, and I instinctively examine the ceiling.

All rise!

"I perceived in this moment," Orwell, the colonial officer, says in his essay, "that when the white man turns tyrant it is his own freedom that he destroys. He becomes a sort of hollow, posing dummy, the conventionalized figure of a sahib. For it is the condition of his rule that he shall spend his life in trying to impress the 'natives' and so in every crisis he has got to do what the 'natives' expect of him. He wears a mask, and his face grows to fit it. I had got to shoot the elephant. I had committed myself to doing it when I sent for the rifle. A sahib has got to act like a sahib; he has got to appear resolute, to know his own mind and do definite things. To come all that way, rifle in hand, with two thousand people marching at my heels, and then to trail feebly away, having done nothing—no, that was impossible. The crowd would laugh at me. And my whole life, every white man's life in the East, was one long struggle not to be laughed at."

An Unfortunate Mishap

During the period in which this book was in preparation, there was a hunger strike involving three thousand convicts in a West Bank prison. The strike ended of its own accord, without the use of force by the prison authority. Lawyers for the strikers were not allowed to meet with them. The prisoners' families were in deadly fear: the methods used for ending hunger strikes in the prisons have acquired a bad reputation.

For example, in 1980 there was a large hunger strike in the Nafha prison. Until that year the prison authority had the practice of giving the prisoners a "subsistence diet"—milk enriched with vitamins, meant to keep them alive. The prisoners themselves agreed to accept this diet, and did not see it as a violation of their strike. In the case of the strike at the Nafha prison, the prison authority decided to physically break the strike: they transferred twenty-one of the strike leaders to the prison in Ramallah, did not give them the subsistence diet, and insisted on pumping the milk directly into the stomachs of the prisoners. The prisoners refused. The medic on duty, an employee of the prison authority named Ruhami (he was later laid off for a morals violation), forced the pipe on some of them, but due to a lack of expertise the pipe entered the lungs of three of the prisoners. The enriched milk filled their lungs and they began to choke.

The lawyer of one of them happened by, and at her insistence her client was taken to the hospital and saved. He died three years later of a heart attack. The other two prisoners suffered all night. Only in the morning were they brought to the local clinic. From there they were sent to the hospital. One died on the way, and the other in the hospital.

A commission set up to investigate "hunger strike practices in the prisons" (the Eitan Commission) examined the circumstances of the deaths of the two prisoners. In their report they "recommended considering their deaths as an unfortunate mishap."

8

Jews Don't
Have Tails

In the heavy fog I almost did not find the village. It was
a white and thick night, and low clouds rose in front of
the car. I searched for the house, but the fog led me
astray into the wrong alleys and sent me over dirt paths.
Then I stopped struggling and allowed myself to travel
at a crawl through the village, and then, for the first
time, I could feel something soft and free before me,
maybe because of the fog lying over the village, maybe
because of the quiet and the late hour; in any case, the
air was completely rid of that thing bitterly called "the
conflict," from the poison of the facts and interpre-
tations and the enmity and the lingering memories. The
Arabs were alone, and I was simply an undetected voy-
eur, and they were without us. From between the scraps
of fog I saw a woman come out toward the doorway of
her house, wiping up the drops of rain with a mop; a
broom seller walked bent over, returning home after
the day's work; in a corner of the street the headlights
of a car lit up the warm secrets of a small grocery store,
where two men sat playing backgammon. It was already

10 p.m. when I found myself outside the Tahers' large house. Taher is not his real name. He asked that I call him that, because the people here are still not willing to listen to his ideas. "Here they want to understand what you think right away: to know whether you are against the occupation or a collaborator and traitor. Black or white. They don't understand that there are several grades in between."

Taher is middle-aged. Somewhat heavy, with glasses, and quick of movement. His speech is swift, a little musical, as if each of his sentences were a question, and movements of his hands illuminate his words with improvised drawings.

He asked me what I had heard from the people I had met in the area.

I told him that only two days ago, in Beit Jala, one public figure told me that if we, the Israelis, were to leave the area, there would be a "second Beirut." The Moslems would slaughter the Christians, and then each other.

Taher answered immediately: "There will be a great slaughter. They will butcher each other on the bridge, anyone who is armed. Afterwards—the others: first they will kill whoever had any connection with Israel, and those who did business with Israel. And those suspected of collaboration with the *mukhabarat*, the intelligence service, and after they kill half of the population here, they will begin killing each other in a struggle for power. But I think"—he smiled—"that if you leave our land, there will be a second Beirut among you as well, because your debate over us, about the territories, is what keeps you from the real disagreements you have among you, which you haven't pursued for twenty years."

And if we stay here, I ask.

"Even if you stay here, it will be the end of you. We are dismembering you from the inside. You are small and want to be a great empire. And as you grow, you will approach your end. Like a child's balloon. And we are gaining strength in the meantime. We have more money, from working for you; we have identity, and that didn't exist before; and we learn many things from you. And today there are many people among us who can send their children to college to study literature and history, as I did—who ever heard of sending a child who can work and bring in money to study, of all things, humanities?"

And if we arrive at some arrangement under which we leave here and you have a government of your own? How do you see the country which will then be born?

He smiles broadly. "That won't be in my time or in yours. It's a dream. If the Jordanians didn't give me a government, do you think that Shamir will? Or Sharon? Peres won't, either. Why waste strength on dreams? Even without that, life is hard for us. Here we live in constant fear that the time is approaching when you will expel all of us from our land. That, after all, is the only difference between your parties, the good ones and the bad ones: when to expel the Arabs. I need all the strength I have in order to live with that fear, and in order to live without freedom, and you ask me about dreams? We need to think only about the possible."

The conversation, by the way, was conducted in Hebrew: twenty days after the Six-Day War began, Taher went to Jerusalem and registered for the intensive Hebrew course at the Beit Ha'am community center. "I knew that the Jews would be here in the West Bank for a long time." How did you know? We ourselves weren't sure that we would. "That's because you still didn't know how much it suits a person to be a conqueror. You thought then that you didn't know how to be like that. But don't forget that I had lived for twenty years under another occupation, the Jordanian, and that I am a much greater expert on conquerors than you are."

And what did your neighbors in the village say when you began to learn Hebrew?

"At first they said *jasus* [spy]. Afterwards, they quieted down and saw the truth."

And what is the truth?

"What I said. That we need to learn from you, and take from you what you can give us.

"If you leave here now and leave us alone—it will be very hard for us." He explained: "You accustomed us to many things, and we aren't what we once were. It would be as if you were to take us to the middle of a stormy sea and say to us: Get along on your own now. We aren't ready for that yet. Maybe in another ten years, twenty years we will be. Not now. And we know that in our hearts—it's just that no one dares say it out loud."

And in the meantime?

"In the meantime, stay with us for a little bit longer. But change your attitude. Change your views. And start thinking about us in a totally different way."

How differently?

"Start thinking about us not as your Arabs, asses that anyone can ride, people without honor. Start thinking about us as your future neighbors. In the end we will be the people with whom you will have to live here and come to an agreement with and create ties with, and do business with, and everything, right? It's not the Japa-

nese you will have to come to an agreement of peace
and trust with, right? Even if there are five more wars
here, the children of my grandchildren and the children
of your grandchildren will finally get wise and make
some sort of agreement with each other, right? So I say:
Change your attitude a little, make some effort in our
direction. Even try—and I know that it is probably hard
for you, right?—try, God forbid, to respect us.

Taher speaks a fluent and special Hebrew. He studied
for three years at the Hebrew University. Then he went
into business. He has extensive links with Israel and his
economic situation is good. Because of his Israeli connections, and because of the things he says, I at first
suspected that he was telling me what he thought I wanted
to hear. I wondered whether he was not deprecating
himself; but I did him an injustice. I wanted to be sure
that I was not mistaken: in the two months I traveled
in the land of Ishmael, I heard once or twice the sickening
sound of the groveler. I was acquainted with the whisper
of one who makes himself a partner in my crime and
tells me: Stay here forever. Only you can save us. You
brought us wealth. Liberty and freedom won't buy us
bread. And this, too: We, the Arabs, need to be treated
with a strong hand. We respect only the person who hits
us. I listened, and tried to find out if the speaker could
say something more than that, about what awaits the
two peoples if the current situation continues, and about
the reality coming into being here. But I heard no more
than the same whispers over and over again. There is
no point in going into details: it does not matter who
said these things—they are said by an enslaved man who

has lost his divine image, and maybe doesn't realize it himself. More than likely he believes what he says with all his heart, but I want nothing to do with such people. You can never trust them. Not when they are under our control and not when we are allied with them.

Taher, however, speaks his own free, original thought, without a trace of groveling or desire to be liked. "Twenty years have passed," he tells me, "twenty years during which we have been together. You already know that Arabs know what theater is, and we know that Jews don't have tails. True, not everyone understands it fully. Sometimes I hear a mother here in the village shout at her child: If you don't eat, I'll tell a Jew to come and kill you! I tell her that she should be ashamed to speak that way, because if you teach your child to fear Jews, you ensure that he will do so all his life, and, after all, he needs to live together with them here, right?"

He speaks with emotion, with urgency. Sweat gathers on his forehead, and his thick eyeglasses fog over, despite the coldness of the large, unheated house. For a moment he looks like a frightened attorney caught between two hotheaded disputants, trying to appeal to what remains of their reason, knowing that if they pounce on each other he will be the first to be crushed.

"You also have much to learn: not to get into our souls, for example. Why do your soldiers need to stop me five times when I go to buy a sack of flour in the main street of Hebron? Why do they need to humiliate me at a roadblock in front of my children, who can see how the soldiers laugh at their father and force him to get out of the car? Of course, you have to behave like conquerors. I don't deny that. That's the way history is:

you won the war and we lost. I say, all right. Be conquerors. Push us, but with delicacy. Because sometimes you push so hard that we see how scared you are."

Scared? Explain that.

"Yes, yes. You should know that you're in a bad position. When I return from Amman, from visiting my brother, and one of your soldiers tells me to undress, and pokes his fingers down there, and checks my underwear, my hair, I look him in the eyes and think, My God, look how the entire Israeli government and the entire Israeli Army are scared of you, Taher. And then you seem to me like a great king who sits in his palace and places many guards around him, but doesn't sleep at night, because he knows that at any minute someone might come and take his crown away."

But you know that our fears are well-founded. We have enemies, we are in danger, and we have to defend ourselves.

"Yes, yes, that's right. But even if you are certainly justified in your searches and your roadblocks and all that—you yourselves feel in your hearts that this is not the right position for you. You want to be great conquerors like the Moslems of Mohammed were, like the Turks and like Napoleon, but on the other hand you want to be merciful and democratic like the English and like America, so what do you do? You make mistakes. Look, every year you have a new political party; anyone with any sense sets up another party, and why? Because no one understands what your country was originally meant to be, and no one remembers what they wanted to do, and believe me, when I sit down with a Jew (and I work with Jews all the time) I feel as if we are both of us in a prison under Israeli occupation."

Then the door opens, and a sleepy child in pajamas comes in, turns to Taher, and jumps into his lap. A small boy, curly-haired, who walks barefoot across the painted floor tiles. Taher speaks to him with movements of his hands, mouthing words for emphasis, and the boy answers with more movements. Taher excuses himself and goes to put the boy to bed. When he returns, he tells me that he has two deaf-and-dumb children. They even studied for a time at the school for the deaf in Jerusalem, but they don't teach Arabic there. He speaks of his children naturally and lovingly, without a hint of reproach in his voice, and I understand without any explanation from him why he so urgently seeks to bring the extremes to reason together, to open their eyes to moderation and caution, and why he cannot surrender to any sort of dream.

9

The Essence of
Being a Sabra

On the way to Kfar Adumim, a settlement just off the Jerusalem–Jericho road, Moni Ben-Ari points to a budding green olive grove to the left of the road and says: "That—that I planted. The people from the JNF laughed and said that nothing would grow, that this is the most barren desert in the world, but I planted anyway. And I'm not a farmer and my father was not a kibbutznik, I was born in Rehavia, in Jerusalem, but I said, They have no choice, these olives, they will grow here."

And afterwards, in his back yard, he leads me among the avocado, pomelo, plum, tangerine, lemon, fig, pomegranate, and orange (one of every variety) trees, and lingers by a young mango tree: "He has to grow . . . no . . . he has no choice . . . you think he has a choice? He has to."

I had wanted very much to meet Moni (Menashe) Ben-Ari. Everyone had told me about him. They told me that he is a real mensch. That's what almost everyone said, as if they had coordinated it in advance: a real mensch.

He is almost forty-five years old, father of four, teacher and settler. His father was Arieh Altman, a member of the Knesset, a Revisionist and one of the leaders of the Herut Party. (Revisionism was a Zionist faction founded by Ze'ev Jabotinsky which called for the establishment of a Jewish state on the entire territory of the British Palestine Mandate; that is, including what is now the Kingdom of Jordan. The Herut Party, founded by Jabotinsky's disciple Menahem Begin, is the Israeli successor to the Revisionist movement.) Moni was at the head of those who founded nearby Ma'aleh Adumim, now the largest Jewish West Bank settlement, and after living there four years under difficult conditions, left to settle in Kfar Adumim. He went out to "this point" (the people of Gush Emunim still speak of "points of settlement," as did the first Zionist settlers of Israel), and here, in Kfar Adumim, established a community settlement of religious and secular Jews together.

Moni, secular, is today a member of the secretariat of Amana, the settlement movement of Gush Emunim; up until seven years ago, he was a member of the executive committee of the secretariat of Gush Emunim, but resigned: "I checked all the time to see if their dreams were in tune with reality. How they come into being. Today I'm no longer part of that [Gush Emunim and its secretariat] for two reasons. The first one is that it is an anti-democratic body. No one elected its leaders, nor did anyone ordain them from above, as a rabbi is ordained. They are not accountable to anyone. It's auto-election. The second thing that sets me apart from them is that, in my opinion, they are a small religious cult, which therefore has no interest in the wider public, and I am a simple Jew from the land of Israel. They're a cult.

They're a *schteibel*. That's not to say that a cult can't be a nice thing. You can meet at night, conduct ceremonies, and read interesting things, have music, but that's not enough to do something on a national level. Something that I would call 'all-Israeli.' That's my personal obsession."

Moni speaks the way Israelis used to speak. Slow, heavy speech with a nostalgia-awakening mixture of slang and Talmud, with those special and characteristic cutoff sentences. Not rude, but tough: "I'd also be happy to see their, the Gush's, bylaws. Some sort of document, anything. Maybe there once was one. I don't know. It'd be interesting to see it sometime. In Amana, though, there's popular rule. General meetings, elections. Organized. And there I work. We settle all over the land of Israel. Here, I'm now advising a new settlement in the Galilee. There are about four groups in the Galilee. Little by little. An acre here, a goat there."

There are eighty families in Kfar Adumim. Four hundred people. There is no friction between the religious and the secular inhabitants. This year they received the Speaker of the Knesset's award for quality of life and tolerance. In the school, everyone wears *kipot* while studying religious texts, but non-religious students are allowed to be excused from studying Talmud and Jewish law, in place of which they learn another subject. People drive on Shabbat within the settlement. It's not co-existence, Moni says; it's existence.

A third of the residents work in the town, in agriculture, workshops, and greenhouses. There is also a horse ranch. The settlers built the houses themselves. They refused to take money from the Jewish Agency. The Agency officials said: We should pay you for going to this mountain, but Moni said that a house is too important a matter for state finance.

"I don't have any dreams about what the future will be. My dreams have been realized already. I even thought that in order to grow artichokes I would have to work down in Jericho. But look, I have them here. What more do I need? Only to progress with Israel as a whole. To create something new here. To absorb immigration. Secular and religious. Ashkenazim and Sephardim. White collar and blue collar. Those are things that you can try to do something with only in a small community. I don't have any other dreams. Only that we grow. That we plant. Listen: they're going to bring Jerusalem sewage here. That will bring water. Don't laugh! Things will be great here, thanks to the sewage.

You, I said, you speak of Israel as a whole. Unity. But Gush Emunim and the settlements over the Green Line have created, for the most part, division and polarization within the nation.

"Here—again I want to talk just about my corner, only about what I'm responsible for. Let's take this place. So, in the first place, it is state land. This whole area is a tract that was never inhabited. And now let's examine what the big boys say about our location. We won't talk about the Likud, just Labor. Labor has talked for years about Jerusalem, afterwards they added 'the Jerusalem area' (and none of the Mapainiks, the old Labor regulars, noticed the change) and the Jordan. Now, if you like, this place is on the Jordan, or if you like, it's Jerusalem. And I, I put the national consensus to the test. National consensus is wonderful. It's democracy, and I like that, democracy, and if we sit down and look at the platforms of most of the parties we can see that according to eight out of ten Jews we are sitting within the national consensus. That's what I understand in life. That is, this nation, on paper, wants this place—and here I am! What, it's not Jerusalem? I can see Mt. Scopus, where I was born, from here, and the Mount of Olives, where my father is buried, he's also a sort of settler there, and the Augusta–Victoria Hospital on the Mount of Olives, which I liberated in the Six-Day War. This isn't Jerusalem? You have to understand, it was Labor that built the army bases at Beit-El and Bamat Givon, and Labor didn't set up bases in places that it didn't think we would serve, right? We need to wait until the people love their entire land—and as for me, I have no problem with the east bank of the Jordan, but the reality is that for now that is something else. And in reality I know exactly where my power ends. I live within my own bounds.

"And if another two or three million of ours were to come here, my appetite would be bigger. But dreams—oho, I'm free of problems in my dreams. The Bashan and the Gilad and the Horan and all those other Biblical places across the Jordan. Do I want them for my people? Of course I want them, what a question! Understand: I didn't say we should conquer them tomorrow! You think that all the great Zionists didn't want the Horan? They wanted it."

I want to understand why Menashe Ben-Ari, a secular Jew, a Sabra like me who was born in Jerusalem, dreams about the Horan.

"Because I have a right to it. What, rights aren't a serious thing? You don't stand on your rights if someone tries to put even something small over on you? We have to demand our rights. Our rights to the Horan were acceptable to the League of Nations two generations ago, not two thousand years ago! In my terms, in my childhood, it's my land, the Horan, yes, I grew up when the British ruled here, and after that there were still books to learn about the land, pictures of the Arnon River and all that, they are my pictures, that is, Jews like me took them, it's Jericho, the Dead Sea, this area here, what are you talking about?!"

And the Arabs who live here?

"Look, it depends how big our country here is, and where we put the borders, but the Arabs who are in this country will be citizens of the country. There's no room for argument—they are citizens here. And as far as I'm concerned, the military government—its time to go has come. Enough. What we need to make now is interim agreements. After all, everything in life is interim. Here, twenty years have passed, so we need to make an agreement. The basis of that agreement will be, first, a wide national consensus, and that the country preserve a large Jewish majority, almost like today, with the addition of relatively uninhabited areas, and a small addition of Arabs in essential areas, and they'll have full rights. Autonomy. And if none of them wants to make a deal with us, we will establish autonomy unilaterally in the heavily populated areas. Not a state. If they make themselves a state, they'll see that someone will take it apart, one-two, with an iron hand. There's no room for another new country between the Jordan and the sea. In my opinion, the most we can give them now is autonomy. Autonomy is not lack of rights. It just doesn't include RPG bazookas, that's all. Now there's the trial of the Nazi Demjanjuk, right? So, in my opinion, what we have to learn from that is that we can't give them RPGs. That's all. If the world wants them to have RPGs, then I'm against the world, what can I do? No wise stuff. And you asked about Hebron. Good, Hebron is a special case from 1929, when the Arabs massacred the local Jewish community. You can't reward slaughter. I think justice is a serious business. There are things you let go and things you don't let go. In the case of Hebron, there are accounts to settle. We have business with them. No one should win a prize for even one successful massacre. Here there is a great account between peoples. History has accounts. And when you return to the old Jewish quarter in Hebron and rebuild the Avraham Avinu synagogue, which the Arabs used as a latrine—that's an answer. When you build and live, that's an answer. Now, I have a lot of criticism about how it was done, I wouldn't suggest going and settling in the middle of Nablus, like they did in Hebron. We don't need anything like that in Nablus. We can settle on the mountain over the city. Above them. Then I'm calm. I feel good. But in Hebron, within Hebron—that's something."

And are historical accounts so important to you today? Are you willing to endanger the present because of them?

"It bothers me. What do you think? I have accounts going back three thousand years. Of my people. I carry them with me. No one asked me before they put them on me. I'm carrying a burden! The only thing I need to think about is what I do with that burden and how I make another generation possible. That's what directs me. If I go to Spain, let's say (I've never left Palestine, you understand), but what do you think, among the Spaniards I wouldn't suffer? Five hundred years of accounts! So there is at least an interesting part to historical accounting, and that's what expelling and destroying us

does to those who hate us: it takes them down several
levels. Look at Germany without all its Einsteins! They
only have Krupp and those types."

So maybe the solution is to leave the territories, hm?
And in that way to take revenge on those who hate us?

Moni laughs his heavy, heart-winning laugh. Outside,
strong winds are blowing from the wadi, from the Syrio–
African Rift. They cry like *shakalim*, jackals, I say, and
meditate that not for nothing did I use the word *shakalim*, like they used to say. Because in a strange way
Moni, among the major initiators of settlements in the
territories, is precisely the man who symbolizes what we
lovingly call "good little Israel." Because he is kibbutz.
And manual labor. And sensuous love of the land without God as an intermediary. Honesty, self-sacrifice, and
simplicity, and also clumsy speech, but of a type backed
up by actions. That, after all, is sabraness, actually, the
essence of concise definition of sabraness, so stereotyp-
ical, to the point that when you meet it, it seems re-
freshing and invigorating. Like a greeting from a world
that no longer exists. And that world already isn't, partly
because of the actions that Moni Ben-Ari himself took
part in. Because of the circumstances he and his friends
brought about, tangling himself into a helpless state.
Very confusing.

"Here, I'll tell you what I tell, say, the guys from the
Peace Now movement who ask me about the settlement
here: I tell them—guys, it's all right, let's see where we
have something in common. How many of you will go
to settle the Negev? How many to the Galilee? How
many of you will decide to be teachers? Simple ones,
second-grade ones, right? How many of your guys will
you require to sign on for the standing army after fin-

ishing compulsory service? Right, right, you'll make them
sign up? How many officers? How many construction
workers? Now, if you won't set up any settlements in
your way—your way, mind you, not mine—if you don't
do anything, then we have nothing to talk about. Nothing. And all your words and all your books and articles—
it's nothing but paper. *Kalam fadi,* like they say in Arabic—words without value.

"And understand: the debate should be the way it was
forty or fifty years ago. It has to be that both sides do
things. In the dispute between the great sages Hillel and
Shammai, we accept Hillel's rulings. Of course. But we
say of Shammai—also the words of the living God. You
can't not settle. But Peace Now, when I see, say, the
Labor Party set up fifty settlements a year in the Negev
and the Galilee with the best of the youth—hoopa! That's
already serious. Then you have someone you can trust.
But that's far off, really far off. Labor doesn't offer anything. And does Peres? He doesn't make settlements.
Doesn't do it. And we do. And it's hard work building
a settlement. And we do one and another one and every
year there is something. And there are people. They
come. You know, it's really startling: I go to Neveh
Ya'akov in Jerusalem, to any apartment, blue-collar
workers sit there: What do you want? We want to set
up a settlement. Hard to believe but that's the way it is.
And they're not from a youth movement and not from
Ben-Gurion and not from flags and not from songs.
There, somehow it comes to them and that's what they
want. And the left—they're in trouble. The whole matter
of unaccountable individualism, of everyone for himself—they're in trouble. We're all in trouble because of
that. Every man for himself is opposed to the instinct

for survival. To the simple instinct for life. And among them—when you get out of the army, they give you money to travel around the world. And they don't have money! And they send the kid for as long as he wants! And then he begins finding himself. And that's all during the ten best years of his life! Between twenty and thirty! Those are the years that you have children and study and develop. What do our sages say? 'At twenty for pursuing a livelihood.' And they—it's a waste of those years, they don't come again. They're not for living out your fantasies in the jungle. They search for pointlessness and become pointless themselves. Finding myself, what am I, those are *kalam fadi*. Horrible nonsense."

Moni talks and outside it grows dark. Actually, it grows purple. Outside the window is a desert void, and past that, brown hills softly joined one to another, contentedly, like the cords of a braided challa, and at twilight they exude a pale amethyst glow. People turn on the lights in their small houses. A point on the mountain. And facing us, through a thin gauze, Sartaba and the eastern approaches of Jericho, and Mt. Ba'al Hatzor and Kiprous, which is the palace Herod built for his mother, and Jerusalem, where Moni was born.

"It really was my dream to see Jerusalem liberated and Jericho and Bethlehem and this place here. I can't deny that. Really a dream. I really wanted that all those years. In my heart. In my head. I had dreams."

I apologize for the next question, silly to my mind, but anyway, it seems to me that I have to ask if—that is—maybe you also laid out, in the secrecy of your room, plans for conquering the city?

"Why is that a stupid question? Listen well: One day, one Jerusalem night, it was two years before the '67 war, what terrible shouts suddenly emerged at eleven at night from Ramban Street in Rehavia, next to my parents' house: 'Moni!!!' I go out, it was Yossi Langotzki, my company commander from my army unit, the son of the first pioneer of the Dead Sea. A Mapainik, from the Labor movement! A Mapainik to beat all Mapainiks, no both-sides-of-the-Jordan Revisionist like me! 'Get down here fast!' Of course I get down there. When Yossi says get down, you get down. I go down in my underwear. He says to me: Listen! I was at Schneller today, at the regiment headquarters, and I said show me the plans for conquering Jerusalem. And they all laughed. Plans? What plans? Where are you coming from? He was in shock. So I was, too. Because I always took it on faith that someone had taken care of that. That is, that someone was looking out for my interests. That's what I believed. Then I didn't know that here you have to do everything yourself. I was naïve. Anyway—I told him, Yossi, that's amazing, what you say. That's not right. I was shaken. He said to me, *Yalla*, come on, let's begin. Do you understand? No one appointed us. It wasn't auto-election, like the people from the Gush. We didn't mean to tell anything to anyone. Just two Jews, civilians from Jerusalem, with maps, notes, whatever; we sat in his apartment, his wife made coffee, and we began to think. Yes. After all, we would be there when they started to shoot. Not anyone else. So there's your answer."

And could it be that today you spend time sitting with someone poring over the plans for the Bashan, for example?

Moni again laughs a slow and warm laugh. "I'm already old. Enough. I only deal with settlement. Now people will come and say that the situation in the ter-

ritories causes corruption. So I state sadly that the corruption existed before, too. It's true, a military government corrupts. We have to get rid of that. Decide one
way or the other. Now, I'll tell you something about
justice. I hate being unjust. It eats away at me if I'm
unjust. But still no one has proven to me that I'm unjust.
The Arab nation is a great nation. Huge. I don't accept
that every two Arabs is a country. The Arab nation is
not a nation without a motherland. Forget that. It has
a tremendous motherland, of which it sees us as just a
part. This people that lives here, the one that calls itself
Palestinian, has not up to the present day realized itself.
And it had many opportunities: it could have realized
itself under the Turks, under the English, under Hussein.
His brothers, no? And I, from the outpost at Notre
Dame, saw what Hussein did to them before the Six-
Day War. How he cut them down with gunfire. What
did we say then? The Arab nation has many motherlands
and countries, and in truth it doesn't bother me that
much. As individuals—of course, a person has a house,
a field, he has rights to that. And if he is a citizen of the
country—he can vote. That's why I don't want two million of them. We'll make an arrangement so that there
will be less than that among us. And whoever belongs
to us is equal. Like me and like you. So I don't say we
should annex tomorrow morning. Because if we do, they
will get the right to vote, but if not—let the noble Arab
nation take care of them. Noble! And by the way, as
long as the gap between the Arab nation's image of itself
and reality is preserved, it is to our benefit."

Moni Ben-Ari does not preach. He explains slowly,
like someone who is figuring out for himself, as he talks,
the facts he presents. Something in the structure of his

face—the crook in the nose, in direct line with his chin—
hints at a personality that always bangs its head against
the wall, and the things he says in such a friendly way
hide in them the hard kernel of the entire conflict: two
nations which still don't recognize each other's legiti-
macy. The Israelis see the Arabs as another branch of
the Arab countries, and the Arabs see us as an artificial
stooge of world imperialism. Dr. Meron Benvenisti argues in this context that any possible solution, of those
now in the air, would be an artificial, political solution
which would not take into consideration the power of
the primal fears, the traumas, the memories, and the
historical accounts, which did not allow either side to
risk even recognizing the other. "And this land," Moni
says, "is very small. How do they say it: Can two kings
sit on one throne? And we are, after all, two beggars.
There isn't even a proverb appropriate to our circumstance. That's right. So we are a beggar who needs to
get along here. Because where can we go? I don't have
another piece of land. Somehow I never learned English,
I learned only about what is here. And as for me, if they
put me somewhere else, I will wither immediately. Only
what is here is mine. Only here."

And what if the government decides that we have to
evacuate Kfar Adumim?

"I will get up and go. Immediately. With horrible
sadness. Understand: I didn't come here for my own
private reasons. I came because I think that my people
need to be here. And I try to persuade others through
what I do here. I told you. An acre here, a goat there.
But if my people decide that they don't want me here—
I will get up and go."

It is already dark. We go out into the garden, and

Moni shows me in the dimness the goldfish pond and the fruit trees, and the young mango tree that has no choice. Moni has four sons; his wife died eight months ago. She is buried in the settlement. That was the completion of the settlement, Moni said: a settlement isn't complete without a graveyard.

The Mountain That Went

I had the privilege of enjoying much help from Nisim Krispil, and I want to thank him. Krispil, an Israeli, once of the Society for the Protection of Nature and the author of many books on nature and outdoorsmanship, spends much time wandering through the West Bank, and in his direct, heart-winning way, establishes immediate rapport with every person. He walks the streets of the West Bank, in the refugee camps and the villages, speaks Arabic like a native, and knows all the smallest customs and manners. During the last few years he has been studying the material culture of the Arabs in Israel and the West Bank in all its aspects—the structure of the villages, the houses, agriculture, traditions and customs, superstitions, and the arts. He calls the Palestinians "the masters of the place," and in his words, they remind him entirely of his forefathers. "We missed a chance to create good relations for the future with the villages here," he says. "We could have built something with them in partnership. In mutual assistance and friendliness. Today, the only people who come to them are people with demands. Teams of surveyors looking for state lands, security police, building examiners, and so on. No one has taken an interest in what can be improved, to distribute clothes to the needy, to bring toys to kindergartens." Krispil himself brings clothes to families he meets, helps out his friends when they have problems with the administration, and performs other small deeds, so simple at first sight, but tremendously valued by the Arabs. He goes everywhere unarmed, even to the most inimical villages. He says that no one has ever tried to hurt him. "Carrying a gun angers the Arabs and humiliates them," he says.

"The occupation," he relates, "has penetrated even the more traditional folklore: for example, there are certain places which have changed their names. The Mt. Gilo range, where the village Beit Jala is located, was once called Ras-Beit-Jala, and today, Jabal-Ma-Rakh (the mountain that went). And there are no few other places which became Ma-Rakh for the Arabs."

Circumstances have also influenced traditional poetry. Nisim gives as an example a traditional gasidah (a long poem, structured according to a classical rhyme scheme and divided into verses), telling of a hunter who hunted a doe and treated it cruelly. Over the last few years, the poem changed, and the hunter became a Jew:

"Pray for our prophet Mohammed/so that he may help you and us./The doe went to graze in the meadows;/the Jew caught her./He chained her;/she began crying for her children./He said to her: Why are you crying, doe?"

The song continues to describe over the course of several additional verses the sufferings of the doe at the hands of the cruel Jew, and in the end an Arab comes to save her. Not only does he save her—he makes the

Jew a surprising proposal: "Lock me in chains instead of her/and free her to her fawns."

And how does it end?

"The cruel Jew saw this./His heart was taken with the nobility of the Arab—and he freed them both."

10

The Other Barta'a

The "situation," like a stage magician, draws another card, links another inseparable ring to the chain. This time it is Barta'a, and actually, the entire problem of the relations of the Arabs of Israel to the Arabs of the West Bank.

The village of Barta'a is situated about three kilometers east of the Wadi Ara valley, between the Israeli cities of Afula and Hadera, in the area called the Little Triangle. The village is built on the two slopes of a ravine called Wadi Elmia, and the huge Kabha clan, with a family tree reaching back to the eighteenth century and inscribed on deerskin, lives here.

The village received its name from Hawali (holy man) Sheikh Muhammad, buried on the mountain peak over the village. Sheikh Muhammad had been a scout in Saladin's army and had participated in the wars against the Crusaders. When he returned from a victorious battle, he would jump with happiness, and they would say of him *bart'a ash-Sheikh*, which means "the Sheikh hopped with joy."

The village was one until 1949. In that year the representatives of Israel and Jordan, meeting in Rhodes, decided that the border between them would run through the ravine that divides the village. It would seem that the drafters of the Green Line saw the ravine their maps indicated as a natural border. It may be that they didn't realize what they were doing.

One morning, the village was divided. Members of the same family and friends and relatives were torn from each other. The village spring remained on the Israeli side, and the mosque in Jordan. Everything was split in two by the sure and powerful hands of maliciously indifferent giants.

During the first years there was no fence between the two countries or between the two villages, but Jordanian and Israeli soldiers prevented free passage of civilians. When the two armies began clashing in this contact area between them, a "proper" border was built. At the insistence of the villagers, a canal was dug to bring water from the spring in Israeli Barta'a to the center of Jordanian Barta'a. The Israelis drank by day and the Jordanians by night. The children in Israeli Barta'a would urinate in the water to taunt their friends on the other side of the border. The women would launch paper boats containing letters to their friends.

The villagers, suffering from longing and frustration, felt their existence split and their lives disconnected. The meanings of so many primal things seemed suddenly to be on the other side of the fence. The two parts of the village did all they could to maintain some sort of illusory fabric of cooperation. Smugglers would bring news from across the border. When Jordanian Barta'a celebrated a wedding, the residents of Israeli Barta'a would stand on the other side of the border and watch the celebration from afar, with binoculars. When a couple married on the Israeli side, the famous singer Abu Leil would arrive from Kufr Qar'a to entertain the guests, and his voice would fill the emptiness of the valley; the Jordanian soldiers on the other side would shoot into the air out of joy. When a child was born in one of the Barta'as, the proud father would station himself on the hill and shout the news across the border with all his might.

Only once, in 1964, did a Jordanian officer allow the villagers from both sides to meet their relatives. The entire divided clan descended into the ravine for three hours and mixed with each other, touched each other, talked without stopping, and cried. It was then that they saw for the first time babies which had been born and couples who had married. One young man from Israel, who had loved a Jordanian girl during the years of separation and had been able to gaze at her only from far off, asked her hand from her father. The *hutba*, the marriage contract, was drafted immediately, and the girl "infiltrated" and came to live in Israel.

Then came the war, the war of 1967, and the border was lifted. The two halves, the two lovers, could finally make their unification a reality. They descended into the ravine, looked at one another—and were strangers.

"We suddenly saw how different they are from us," Riad Kabha, the young mukhtar of the Israeli village, said to me during my visit there. "We had been with the Israelis for nineteen years. We were more modern than they were, more open and free. It was hard for us to get used to them. Their internal rhythm was different. The whole way they thought about things was different. For example, our attitude toward women is liberal and advanced,

and with them there was—and is today—complete separation of boys and girls from school age onward, and
equality between the sexes is not even a subject for discussion. Along with that, we felt that they somehow looked
down on us. As if they had remained more faithful to tradition and to Islam. They would lecture us haughtily,
feeling that they were better Arabs than we were.

"Contact with them was awkward and unpleasant.
They had been all that time under oppressive Jordanian
rule, and their links with the outside world had been
extremely limited. Jordanian soldiers lived among them
and intimidated them; they were trained to say 'yes, sir'
and 'no, sir' and it affected their entire behavior. Our
Barta'a, the Israeli one, was richer and more active. Our
houses were more luxurious, and every family lived on
its own. With them, a married son would continue to
live with his father. People pay less attention to their
fathers' advice among us, and every person sets out on
his own. Individualists. Even in daily life there are differences: they go to Tulkarm and Nablus for shopping
and enjoyment, and those cities are their focal point in
every way. Our focus is the Jewish city of Hadera. There
is a gap and there is distance between us."

In 1971, a young man from Jordanian Barta'a de-
scribed the young people on the Israeli side as follows:
"They are shallow politically. They do not have a serious
foundation for understanding current events and lack a
proper outlook for the future. They are influenced out-
wardly by the Jewish people; they took the shell of modern society and threw away the content. They do not
have strong family connections. They change their opinions as the situation changes, and they have no principles."

Riad Kabha's comments on this criticism were in a way defensive and apologetic. "We have not taken only the shell of the modern world," he said. "We have taken more than that. We have many positive characteristics—higher social awareness; we are more active than they are, better able to organize ourselves in order to help ourselves, and in the framework of the political problems, we do everything possible in order to . . ."

Kahba continued to speak, and it was possible to guess in advance what he would say and how he would say it. He is a nice person, wise and moderate, and he is caught, to his sorrow, in the trap that captures every uprooted person. He has abandoned one way of life without having absorbed another. People like him speak very carefully: they are well acquainted with the tenuousness of uncompromising statements untested by threats and temptations. I supposed that in the other Barta'a I would hear more uncompromising, determined, strong language, but Riad Kabha and the people of Israeli Barta'a had personally felt how life can erode the totality of the ideal, and of natural, primal aspirations.

The other Barta'a (the people of each call their sister village "the other Barta'a") winds up the face of the ravine, and is poorer and more crowded. Lines of cactus break through the fences of each house, and herds of sheep kick up dust in its alleys. 'Amar Kabha notices me talking with some teenagers in the street, and suggests I come with him to his house. He is twenty-six years old, but looks much older. He works in the poultry slaughterhouse in Hadera, and does nicely. His new house is large and sunlit, built like the houses in Israeli Barta'a.

His small children play on the floor mats, and there is a wide, open view from the window.

"I was a boy when the village was reunited. I remember not knowing my grandmother until the reunification. Other children had grandmothers and I was jealous. I would run over the hill facing the other Barta'a, and I would call out "*Siti Siti*, Grandmother" to every old woman I saw there, but I didn't find her. When my grandfather died, we learned about it from hearing the shouts and wails from the Israeli side. My father could not go to his funeral, of course.

"Every so often, the Israeli authorities would bring a movie to the other Barta'a, and the people there, with us in mind, would project it on the side of a house that faced us. I remember how we would bring benches and chairs and sit out at night to see those movies. They were very popular among us, at least as much as Egyptian President Nasser's speeches on television."

"*As-salam and aleikum.*"

Judat and As'ad, friends of 'Amar's, enter the room. They are also, of course, of the Kabha clan. Judat, tall, curly-haired, delicate-featured, studied economics at Irbid University in Jordan. He cannot find work in his profession here: "I worked for a while in a pub in Tel Aviv, and I spoke to Israeli students there. They studied exactly the same material I studied. Afterwards, I worked as a dishwasher in a restaurant. Until I couldn't stand it anymore—they paid me so little, and treated me like a servant—so I came back to the village. You're surprised? We have an Oxford-educated engineer here who works picking oranges and repairing cars. We have some street cleaners with college educations. I know a dish-washer who has a master's degree in economics. Can you imagine how someone like that feels? We made a mistake when we went to college. We had great aspirations, and we forgot where we come from. Our parents spent their life's savings on us, sold their herds in order to pay for our studies, and we come back to the village, no longer really belonging here. But they won't accept us anywhere else. I sit and read newspapers all day, hang out with my friends, and grow older."

I ask him if he knows what the people in Israeli Barta'a think of them. He laughs and says, "You talked with them, didn't you? You tell me." I say that on my way here I recorded an unflattering description of them from an Israeli Arab, a native of nearby Um el Fahm. I qualify it in advance by saying that it is very derogatory, on the most general level, but authentic nevertheless. "Imme-diately after the war," the young Arab told me, "without even waiting for the cease-fire, we all ran to Barta'a. All those years we had heard the adults talking about how Barta'a had been cut in two, and about the wonderful people there, and we wanted to see for ourselves. So what did we see? A filthy village. People dressed shab-bily, in clothes from twenty years ago. We had bell-bottom pants, they had straight-legs. When we started wearing straight-legs again, they started wearing huge bell-bottoms. We, when we got older, didn't grow mus-taches. They all have mustaches two meters long! We had a game when we were kids of counting the mus-taches of *dafawin*, that's what we call them, *dafawin*, you know, people who live in the *dafa*, the West Bank, and every Arab will put down the Arabs of the West Bank Barta'a by saying, 'What a *dafawi!*' "

"It's not a serious study of us," Judat says, "but simple things like that really do reflect a lot. When we met Israeli Arabs, and from the other Barta'a in particular, they thought we were simply backward. Like the Negroes in Africa, for instance. They still like to think they are better than us, but there are statistics, and they say that there are more high-school graduates among us, and more college graduates. Maybe the conditions of the occupation are what keep us from making the most of our abilities; after all, the whole world knows that the Palestinians have great potential, knowledge, and experience of life. Israeli Arabs have already lost that gift, that 'spark.' They have become spoiled and rotten. Their thinking is already lazy. So they have color televisions and I have only a black-and-white, and he eats meat every day and I have meat only once a week. He thinks that's culture, but he is wrong. Israel improved their standard of living a great deal, but their minds have gone to sleep. Maybe it's because they try very hard not to think of their complex predicament, so they busy themselves with unimportant things: they spend their lives competing with their neighbor over standard of living and external wealth. The most important thing for them is who can build their son a house first. It's the opposite with me. I have a sixteen-year-old brother. He could get married tomorrow, but I won't let him: he needs to finish his studies first. To build his life. And another thing—we are better than them when it comes to human relations. Israel was a bad influence on them in that area as well. Friends and relatives aren't as close. They've become like the European Jews among you"—he laughs—"and we've stayed like the Middle Eastern ones."

'Amar: "When we go there for a wedding, they laugh

at us. 'They've come to get some food!' And afterwards they laugh and say, 'The *dafawin* came and ate everything!' They say they're just joking, but we know they mean it."

As'ad (twenty years old, baby-faced, works in the village, getting married next month): "They have Israeli identity cards, so they can go to Tel Aviv and hang out all night and no one does anything to them. I have to return to the village at night, or hide if I want to sleep there. My car has the blue license plate of a *dafawi*, and they have yellow Israeli plates. They feel like kings because of that, because the police will stop me at a roadblock and let them pass, like Israelis. Once I was driving along the road and the car behind me honked the whole time so that I would get off the road and let him pass. I looked in the mirror and saw an Israeli Arab. It didn't help me any—he almost threw me off the road, and as he passed he even shouted, 'Move aside, move aside, you dirty *dafawi*, go back to Nablus where you came from!' "

The other two nod their heads.

As'ad: "If you ask out a girl from there, she says, 'I don't go out with *dafawin*.' "

'Amar: "Still, there have been some marriages with them during the last few years. At first they didn't want to, but now they're getting used to it."

As'ad: "It's like an Ashkenazi Jew not wanting to marry a Yemenite Jew."

'Amar: "And there's something interesting. Whenever they have a fight with someone over something, they run to us and ask us to fight for them."

The three of them laugh. "As if we were their bodyguards."

Riad Kabha from Israeli Barta'a confirms this with an awkward smile. "In 1972 the Israeli border guard wanted to fence off part of our land for training. We didn't know what to do. We sat and talked about it. People from the other Barta'a, the Jordanian one, suddenly appeared, and asked us, What are you planning to do about it? We said, We'll shout, we won't let it pass quietly, we'll have a press conference! They laughed at us and said, Come out to the land itself and we'll fight. We fought together with them. They came and lay down in front of the bulldozers. They had a lot more nerve than we did."

Judat: "They always brag about how much like the Israelis they are, yet they don't sense what the Israelis think of them. Israeli Arab towns like Faradis and Kufr Qar'a don't get the same kind of government support Jewish settlements get. Here a week ago the government decided that the Druse and Circassian communities would be granted equal rights with the Israelis. They're not giving equality to Israeli Arabs. I don't envy them—they don't have any pride. They only take things from the country, but they don't do anything for it. While you do reserve duty forty-five days a year, they go to the beach. If I were in their position, I wouldn't take anything from the country at all—not social security, not social benefits, nothing."

I read them what the young man from Um el Fahm told me: "They'll tell you how miserable we are and how much Arab pride they have. Sure! We were in Israel twenty years, and we collaborated with you a little, but not excessively, and never of our own volition. They did. True, there were some among us who sold you land, but you took most of our land by force. And here they came, the *dafawin*, and within a year or two they had sold land, received weapons from you, collaborate with you even more than you need them to, maybe! They look down on us? They haven't suffered a tenth of what we have! They took all our lands. We suffered horrible oppression under the military government before 1966. And them? What do they know? They can travel freely wherever they want. At the most they get stopped at a roadblock here and there. And I'll give you one small example why I hate the *dafawin*: once an Israeli took his cigarettes out of his pocket and offered them to me and to a *dafawi*. I said no thanks and nothing more. The *dafawi* kissed the Israeli's fingers and said he didn't smoke. Kissed his fingers! That's the difference between us."

'Amar, Judat, and As'ad listen and laugh derisively. Judat says: "They suffered more than us? How many years did they live under a military government and how many years have we lived under one? And with us there's no end to it in sight! They talk about oppression? What do they know about oppression? They say we sold land? Sure, there are some who sell land, and there are others who sell their souls . . ."

The three of them talk together excitedly, interrupting each other in an odd, almost Jewish, competition over how much they had suffered at the hands of the Jews. Judat adds: "They cry about being second-class citizens. But the truth is that they are fifth-class citizens!" The three West Bank Barta'ans give me their ranking of all those who live under Israeli sovereignty: first come the Jews, who are first-class citizens. Then come the Jewish immigrants from Ethiopia, who are second-class. Then come the Bedouin, and then, they say, we come, because we lack rights but we have pride, and at the very end come the Israeli Arabs.

"Understand," says Judat, "that in living here, in the West Bank, I constitute an international problem. The whole world talks and argues about me. No one talks about him. I am free in my soul, I know that I can say what I feel toward you and the occupation with a full heart. He can't. He is too tied up with you. He can't even think about it. He prefers not to think about it."

As'ad: "That's why they feel uncomfortable when they meet us. They suddenly have to decide who they really are."

'Amar: "They call themselves Israeli Arabs, but they don't call us Palestinians, because that is problematic for them. They call us West Bank Arabs or just *dafawin*. Their children even talk that way—instead of saying, 'I'm going to the other Barta'a,' they say, 'I'm going to the *difa*,' to the West Bank."

Riad Kabha, the mukhtar of Israeli Barta'a, said of that: "They really see themselves as part of the Palestinian people. We see ourselves as part of the Palestinian people, but also as an integral part of Israel. The sad part about it is that the Israelis reject us because we are Arabs, and the Arab countries reject us because we are Israelis. The Arabs in the other Barta'a continue to see us as part of Israel. But despite that, if you write about us, you should write the whole truth: in recent years the differences between us are starting to blur. After all, twenty years have passed. There are more marriages between them and us. There is more contact. They are beginning to be a bit influenced by our way of life. We've also gained something: our national consciousness has grown stronger as a result of contact with them. As if we had remembered our roots again. Our economic superiority could not stand up to their political superiority."

"If, in the future, they ever decide to set up a Palestinian state," said the young Arab from Um el Fahm, thirty years old, university graduate, now living and working in Jerusalem, "and if Um el Fahm were to be included in that Palestinian state, I would not want to live there under any circumstances. You have to understand that I was educated here. My way of thinking is from here. I'm already used to this life, even to our special status among you, on this quarter-democracy you have given us. Do you think I could go now and live with them in Nablus?"

Just before I left West Bank Barta'a I met a young, embittered man who works as a laborer in Israel. After asking that I not print his name, he told me: "If we act like fools, the gap between us and Israeli Barta'a will always remain. If we are smart, we will learn it all from them. There are lots of things worth taking from them. The future lies in their direction, not in ours. Look how they enjoy life, and what dogs' lives we have. With us, the father decides everything, and he doesn't always understand how life has changed. Their women study, ours don't. Among us, a father has many children, so they all remain poor generation after generation. With them, every family has three children and stops. A guy my age and with my intelligence who lives there will succeed more than me, and will be happier. But if we are smart, if we learn from them exactly what they learned from you, when you come here twenty years from now, you won't see any difference between Barta'a and the other Barta'a."

11

Swiss Mountain
View—A Story

Gidi raced lightheartedly up to the edge of the village, where he slowed the pace of his gasping Peugeot truck, and turned calmly and considerately onto the main road. It was early afternoon and only a handful of villagers were out in the street, and they nodded at him in a slightly summary way. Gidi was a little disappointed, because he expected that they would be happier to see him: he had not been there for six weeks. He supposed, however, that they were waiting to find out what his extended absence and sudden return meant for them.

He stopped by Al-Sa'idi's small grocery store, checked routinely to see if his pistol and case of maps were on him, pushed his sunglasses up above his forehead, locked the car, jiggled the key in the lock—and just performing those actions filled him with a feeling of power and joy.

"Abu Dani! *Ahlan*, Abu Dani!" The storekeeper, small and quick to serve, called out to him, went out to greet him, dragged him inside, and seated him on a stool. "Sit, sit. We haven't seen you for so long!" At the crook of a finger a small, barefoot boy hurried behind a filthy curtain to make coffee.

Gidi looked over the shelves and smiled at Al-Sa'idi: "How's business?"

Al-hamdu-lla. And where have you been, Abu Dani? It's been maybe a month that we haven't seen Abu Dani.

Work.

The storekeeper bared yellow teeth and laughed, as if party to some dark secret:

Your work—I won't ask any questions!

The coffee arrived. They drank.

He didn't want to spend too much time here, with Al-Sa'idi, in the unlit store. He was too happy right now to waste his time here, and wanted to be in the light, at the top of the hill, taking in the view. He wanted to shout what he had to say to the whole world. But he didn't mean to start in Al-Sa'idi's grocery. Not that it mattered to him that Al-Sa'idi know in the end, too—after all, everyone would know—but his heart stilled for a split second when he imagined himself telling Al-Sa'idi first. Even though Gidi liked him and was grateful to him, because this crafty little storekeeper had been the first one to dare offer Gidi a cup of coffee, when he came to the village after the war, to work.

Gidi had been young and inexperienced then, just through a crash course put together to provide for the immediate needs of the war, and was sent out to fend for himself. When he came to the village, six years ago, at the end of '67, his muscles had been a frozen lump of fear and tension. He had caught his reflection in the window of the Peugeot and had seen his shoulders bunched up almost to the level of his ears. The villagers followed his movements with concern, not with enmity. From the way he walked, they could identify immediately who he was. They had endured not a few years of occupation under the Jordanians and had already been under the thumb of people like him; he slipped easily into the territories they had evacuated in their souls to make room for deference and inaction.

He told them that his name was Abu Dani, "the father of Dani," Arab custom being to call a man by the name of his eldest son. They would often send regards to his Dani, and he answered them with a smile and invited Allah to bestow his blessings on their children. Over the course of the years, he came to know them all: the children, the grandchildren, and the great-grandchildren. As he passed through the streets of his village, he would feel a slight bureaucratic throb of satisfaction, of a type he had never known, like a shopkeeper examining the merchandise in his store.

The basic work had been hard, and there had not been anyone to help or instruct him: all the senior members of the unit, all the instructors from the course, were busy those days gathering and absorbing the endless intelligence that victory brought with it: documents and people, suspects and collaborators, cities and villages to be utterly penetrated, to crack the code of relations and alliances and allegiances of the people, the leaders, the clans, a great quiltwork, intense study, no holds barred—knowledge is power.

Everything had to be brought to light quickly, before the people had a chance to think twice, before anyone had an opportunity to apply counterpressure: family ties, acquaintances, intimate friends, letters, secrets, diseases, hidden defects, all types of perversions—Gidi worked tirelessly in those days, in a fever, grabbing the village from the underside, exposing it to the sunlight, knowing that he had to hurry and preserve what he found out, before the sun had a chance to parch the delicate, bashful frescoes he uncovered.

Six years. Three thousand people. He knows almost all the men by their full names. He can recite in his sleep the number of children Hashem Al-Masri has, and the names of all of Fa'ad Abu Saliman's creditors; nowadays he barely needs to exert himself here, today he is already responsible for three additional villages, but he keeps a warm place in his heart for his first one. Proof: he came here immediately when his vacation ended. Here he wants to break his news for the first time. A sort of slightly foolish gesture of thanks, but it is that naive, unprofessional foolishness that makes him tremble slightly.

A quiet village, Gidi thought, walking again in the sunlight, greeting the vegetable man, shaking hands here and there, regaining the authoritative gestures of his job. An easy, dignified walk, so different from the way he walked in Israel, and belying the wild joy he felt inside, which he felt he must bellow, roar.

Nimr, ten years old, rolling an iron hoop with a stick, almost ran into him, and was aghast. A nice boy, Nimr, and Gidi felt like his godfather: when Nimr was small and suffered from kidney disease, Gidi saw to it that he was operated on at the Hadassah Hospital in Jerusalem. It was in that way, using such simple and humanitarian means, that he succeeded in winning over an entire clan. Gidi smiled at Nimr and winked, and the little boy made off on his way, rolling his hoop and trumpeting. Gidi made a mental note to talk to Nimr's father about his cousin, Aref, who had traveled to Amman three times in the past year. And another detail he had meant to find out about before leaving suddenly on his long vacation: Is Bassam Abaida still meeting his beauty in Hebron? Unimportant details, which will be of use someday.

My Arabs are quiet, Gidi reflected, I can leave them for a month and a half, and they stay quiet. In other places there are always disturbances, but in my village it is always quiet, and that is because I know how to handle them.

He walked past two women drying watermelon seeds on a blanket, joked with a few construction workers who were setting up a scaffold, exchanged macho jibes with them, and shook their brown, hard hands. They asked him where he had disappeared to, and he was almost tempted to tell them, but stopped himself, because he felt that the first time he wanted to tell it differently; he didn't know exactly in what way it would be different. Maybe—with more festivity. In any case, he had a feel for how he did not want to say it. And he did not want to now. That is—not to them.

It was a hot, good day, full of shining light. Gidi strode through the street, his hands behind his back, lost in his thoughts, greeting with a nod of his head the figures appearing before his eyes. The long separation from the village—the longest since he began working here—gave him a more disinterested and slightly celebratory way of looking at his work, and everything that had happened recently in his life made him—so it seemed to him—wiser and more mature; he reflected on how easy it was for him to control this large population, he had almost never needed violence to do it, and with the exception of one or two cases of discontent and shouting, the villagers had helped him perform his job in a dignified way.

They would come to his office in the next district over and report to him all he requested, almost without opposition and without enmity, as if humoring the unpleasant eccentricity of an insistent relative. During tense times he would tighten his hold on them a little, and when the tension passed, he would let up. He was always on guard, but was amazingly good at hiding it. They did not sense it, and he also trained himself to live with his guard up, though invisible, so that it wouldn't interfere with his private life. He never forgot, though, that he was in enemy territory, and the news which flowed out of the teleprinter did not allow him to forget. Terrorist cells were active everywhere, performing cruel, animal-like deeds, and he and his colleagues were the main buffer against them. Without their work, there would not be a minute of peace either for the Israelis or for his tranquil Arabs. Gidi began his job as a professional, and stayed with it as an idealist.

Over the course of those four years, Gidi spread his net wisely over the village. He preferred to see it as a commercial venture in which the villagers provided information and in exchange gained security, as well as the licenses and permits they needed. Gidi tried not to force anyone to provide information. But every villager needed, along the way, various documents, building permits, or permission to cross the Jordan bridges, so that they had to go through Gidi's modest office and talk with him over a cup of coffee.

I've studied them, he told Billie when he met her four years ago, I study them the way you study Hebrew, a new language. With all the fine points and nuances. When you know a language well, you can suddenly make out when something isn't right. In what way? Billie asked. So that I can feel even the smallest change in my village. Any tension. Or if a stranger appears. Billie, who was smart, asked: The question is whether you understand it for real, from inside, or whether you only know how to press a button and get your output, like, say, from a machine, right? And Gidi, who was an honest young man and did not ever allow an illusion to lead him astray, and who was cruel in his demands on himself, was thrown off by her comment, and turned it over and over without finding an answer to it.

There were also villagers who showed up at his office without having been invited. Sometimes in order to report something about their neighbors, or about their enemy in the village, and sometimes they just came in order to sit with him for fifteen minutes, drink coffee, and make up a story. The grocery-store owner was one of those. At first Gidi thought they were coming to look him over, to feel out his intentions, but after a while he realized foggily that there were people who had some strange compulsion to be around him. To expose themselves to a vague temptation which he embodied for them.

But most of the villagers came to him only at his behest. He scheduled appointments, and arranged it so that every year he would meet all the adult males living in the village. It entertained him to think that they themselves knew nothing of his clever planning and could not guess what role each of them played in the picture as a whole. They would sit with him for a short time, try to satisfy him, embarrassing him a little by treating him like a father. Like someone older than they, experienced and very powerful. It was necessary for him to adjust himself to a small change in his internal image of himself when he crossed the Green Line which separates Israel from the West Bank, and again became Gidi. They would tell him with quiet, choked voices all he wanted to know. They in any case felt that he knew everything about them, about their public and private lives, and they had already stopped wondering which of their friends had given him that particular piece of intimate information about them. They could no longer trust anyone, not even members of their families, and that made them even more submissive and apathetic than they had been six years before. He himself noticed that for a long time they had not been able to tell him anything he did not already know, and he somehow felt that they had given him all the information they had and their whole selves as well.

But he did not want—he really did not want—to think of those kinds of things on this wonderful summer morning, as he strode among them, bursting with happiness, looking for the one person worthy of being told of the birth of his first son, slightly disappointed to discover that all of these old acquaintances of his had become somehow transparent and hollow, as if they were all very old or very childish, and that none of them was his age: that is, not really his age, but, how to put it, close to him. That is—a sort of uneasiness came over him. And impatience.

Gidi never believed that they hated him for what he did to them as part of his work. He was sure that they knew how to appreciate his delicacy, the respect he showed for them. Not like certain colleagues of his who accomplished their work through the use of overt and covert power and violence. Gidi did not need that, and was happy for it. Only once, about two years ago, he had had to make small use of the "starling" procedure on one of the village teachers, who had suddenly turned into a young and disgruntled "crow," darkly shrieking. Gidi warned him a few times, surprised him with an exact quote of things he had said to his pupils during a Koran lesson, and explained to him reasonably what those things would lead to. The man refused to take the hint. He had a bitter soul and was full of hate, and blasted Gidi with strident words, so strange to the spirit of the tacit and unwritten agreement Gidi had with the village. Gidi really had no choice but to use the "starling" procedure. It was almost fun to see in actual use a simple and subtle exercise from the course. Officers, friends of Gidi's who had borrowed senior officers' insignia, would arrive in luxurious military cars, not the usual trucks, and would invite themselves to lunch at the house of the "crow." At the end of the meal they would ask him to show them out, and outside the house, in front of everyone, they would slap him on the back and shower him with smiles and winks. The village was soon muttering and giggling. It had been necessary to direct the matter wisely and with great sensitivity. Not to awaken a real uproar against the teacher, but only to ostracize him. Within two weeks the pupils in the crow's class were boycotting his lessons, and a month later he took his wife and four children and moved to another village. Eviatar, Gidi's colleague there, reported that the man was quiet. He became a canary.

Someone ran and called out after him. Gidi turned around. The village elder, the mukhtar Harbi, ran after him, calling him with a smile, his feet getting tangled in his robe. Gidi thought—Here, this is the man I will tell, with him it feels right. He waited without moving until the mukhtar approached him, obeying an unwritten law that the villager must approach the officer and not the opposite, and then he shook his hand, gripping it with determination, in order to keep the slightly excited man from falling on his face.

The mukhtar pelted him with questions, his words running into each other in emotion: where had Abu Dani been, why had he suddenly disappeared, had he come back for good, the village had been very worried, they sent some other officer, not as nice as Abu Dani, we were getting scared he would stay here, and he didn't want to tell us where Abu Dani had gone, we thought Abu Dani didn't love us anymore—the man chuckled, pulling Gidi toward his house—after all, he can't go without having coffee with Harbi, who almost didn't sleep at night worrying about him, because Abu Dani is like a brother to him; what do I mean brother, son.

With a certain reluctance Gidi allowed the heavyset, heavily clothed mukhtar to lead him toward his house. He would really rather have remained in the sun, in the clean light, filling up with the clear air, but he knew that he could not refuse Harbi, and not only that, he had already returned to work, and would have to sit with Harbi anyway and hear what was new in the village.

The house was large and handsome. They sat in the light-filled living room, sinking into the greenish velvet armchairs, smoking the Israeli Time cigarettes that the mukhtar saved specially for Gidi. He would always open him a fresh pack and Gidi was somehow flattered by that: a sort of personal gesture.

So, where was Abu Dani all this time?

He gazed at the brown, large face gazing at him from close range, baring before him its lines in a too open way, intimate and embarrassing. Over the last six years Gidi had seen those lines rearrange themselves into varied and different expressions—he had seen deep, heart-rending fear, desperation without hope; he had seen them cry, and seen them greatly calmed. Sometimes he thought he saw sincere, instinctive affection as well, affection which transcended the limitations of circumstances. The first few times, he saw the mukhtar Gidi was very impressed with the man's nobility. He was like a legendary Arab hero. Afterwards he began liking him as a person, not as a legend: the mukhtar was an emotional and stormy man, and knew how to win Gidi's heart. Gidi was thankful to him, because he had given him, actually, the key to the riddle of many of the villagers.

Your health is all right? the mukhtar asked, worried by Gidi's silence. Is the family okay? The children? How is your Dani?

Sometimes, and especially during the past month, when he had spent much time at home with Billie, Gidi had reflected on his previous life, after he left the army, and before he began his new work. He told Billie that he thought he had once been much more naive. Really, I was so naive, he told her, his hands running over the long brown hair spread out around her head, and she said: "You? Naive?" and laughed the short, nervous laugh that she had made her own during the last months of her pregnancy, and said that she was sorry she had not known him then. You were probably nicer, she said, and she pouted, slightly resentful.

Gidi did not want to start another argument with her, so he only smiled and was silent, but he thought to himself that people once seemed much better to him than they really are. Much more proud and interesting and natural. I really did live in an incubator at the kibbutz, he thought, embarrassed at remembering his immaturity then, and the things he used to write to his previous girlfriend, stupid ideas about how in every man there is a riddle that makes him special and different, some deep-forged secret . . . I was like a kid, he thought, a kid who looks in from outside at the adult world.

I had things to do for work, Gidi blurted out in the end at the earnest face of the mukhtar.

Ah! About work I don't ask any questions! Work!

And the mukhtar leaned back, wearing a discreet expression, almost a caricature.

And will Abu Dani stay here with us? We're the only ones for him, right?

The only ones. And from now on, everything will be like it used to be.

Ah, good. That's very good. Very good.

The coffee arrived, and the mukhtar told Gidi about the grape honey he plans to concoct this year, and about his intestinal troubles, and about Fufu, the village eunuch and idiot, who had suffered an epileptic fit and had been taken to the hospital and had almost died there. Yes, Gidi thought, suddenly having a hard time keeping himself within the shower of the man's chatter, today I know people for what they are. Work taught me a lot, no question about it. They have no secret and no riddle. If anyone can be sure of that, I can. Because they tell me their most hidden thoughts. And I see them in their most intimate circumstances. They have no mystery. They are so predictable and banal. And what moves them, always, is just a few simple, miserable urges: the same fears, the same appetites, and they are really nothing but machines, really, machines without independence and without souls, so easy to operate and direct according to one's needs.

The mukhtar told him the latest news. Gidi listened and filed it away in his memory. Suddenly he asked about Abu Khatem, and saw how the mukhtar's face went yellow with repugnance. Leave Abu Khatem alone, the mukhtar said. They sipped their coffee in silence. Abu Khatem was the richest man in the village. He had little to do with the rest of the villagers, nor did he allow his wife and two children to talk too much with the neighbors. There was a sort of mystery about him, but no security risk. Gidi visited his house once or twice and felt uncomfortable there. The mukhtar sighed, and said that nothing was new with Abu Khatem, no one visits him, and he doesn't leave his house, and why did Abu Dani have to bother himself about him.

Gidi rose abruptly, almost rudely, bade the mukhtar goodbye, and went out. The air was transparent and clear, but still lacked something to expand the lungs. Gidi walked along the path that went up the side of the mountain, kicking stones and picking bunches of yellow and white daisies, only to throw them away. He had surprised himself by his hurried exit from the mukhtar's house, but he had suddenly felt himself suffocating there. He thought about the child born to him two days ago, his first child, and he was not filled with happiness. A boy leading a few black, scrawny goats passed him and greeted him with deference, and Gidi glanced at him angrily and did not answer. He reflected on the fact that things which once seemed to him to be the most basic principles of a moral life—honesty and courage and self-respect—now seemed pathetic hypocrisy. Courage was only fear that had not been put to the test. Honesty was only deceitfulness that had not had to face temptation. All noble virtues were now in his eyes only signals which pointed the observer to their opposites, their ruin.

Almost without meaning to, he knocked on Abu Kha-tem's door, not understanding why he had come there. He had, after all, always tried to refrain from going to this house and to this rich, reclusive man. Abu Khatem possessed something that demanded a different attitude from Gidi, quieter and more subtle, and Gidi had always felt that he did not want or could not respond to that demand. The mistress of the house opened the door, and her expression cooled at the sight of him. She led him into the dimly lit living room, curtained on all sides. He sat in an armchair and admired the carved amber columns and heavy chandeliers. A huge Swiss mountain view, complete with a peaceful stream, a snow-covered alp, and greenery, covered the entire wall opposite him.

The master of the house entered, tall, thin, and dark, like a magician's hat. Two small children defiantly peeked out at Gidi from the hallway. The woman served tea. Gidi waited for the man to say something and break the silence, but Abu Khatem did not open his mouth. Gidi was forced to speak, and found himself mumbling trivialities. Abu Khatem answered curtly. Gidi knew that the man had not left his house for six years, and had barely seen the sun. The villagers did not know how to explain the change that had come over him: even before the war, they said, he had not been a sociable man, but he would leave the village and return, talk with people, and people even remembered that he knew how to joke. Now it was as if he had placed an interdict on the village and denied himself to the villagers. Maybe he holds them in contempt, Gidi thought in a flash. How did I not see that before, maybe he holds them in contempt because they are so miserable and docile, he thought, and suddenly he felt a strange surge of compassion for this stern-faced, ascetic man sitting silently opposite him, a sort of pleasant burning sensation in the depths of his lungs, as if something of the Swiss mountain air from the great wall picture had made its way into them, and he asked the man about his elderly father in Jordan, and expressed his surprise that Abu Khatem did not submit a request to visit Amman, or to allow his father to visit here. After all, it is pretty easy to arrange something like that, and everyone does it, and Abu Khatem said he was not interested, nor was his father, and Gidi, who now felt very close to this silent, proud man, decided that he would not leave this house without persuading Abu Khatem to submit a request for a visit. Get out a little and get some air, he said with an odd enthusiasm, see how the world has changed, see that we've given you some good things, too, and anyway, your father is not a young man, it's worth seeing him because, who knows, and you are his only son, right, you see, I remember everything, and to be an only son is a special thing, I can say that with certainty, because when you have a son—and Gidi almost felt for a split second the precise joining of the desire and the necessity to tell his news, finally, to someone here, to one of the thousands under his management, those into whose lives he had been prying for six years and with whom he had drunk thousands of cups of coffee and tea. And here, with Abu Khatem, he really felt that he wanted, had to tell, tell and hear how it sounds out loud and in Arabic, even though were he to say it he would reveal finally that there was no previous son named Dani, and his relations with the village would go through a sort of clarification and purification, but something nevertheless stopped him, maybe the expression of warning, disapprobation, and enmity on the man's face, or the knowledge that Abu Khatem would not even get up to shake his hand, and the news would remain hanging in the air, deflated, and Gidi quickly sat up straight, bid the master of the house goodbye, and left even before they rose to accompany him, and feeling as if he had been expelled. He descended swiftly from the hill, resentful and angry, acknowledging in spite of himself the unquestionable nobility of Abu Khatem, the natural and annoying authenticity he possessed, something which reminded Gidi of his father, of all people, and he hurried to his truck, passing along the way villagers who greeted him with weary gestures, now seeming to him without any life or sincerity, and he returned them an angry wave, feeling like an art collector who has filled his warehouses with cheap forgeries and has just seen the originals.

He tore out of the village, pressing the gas pedal of the Peugeot to the floor, as if fleeing from an infected place, but not really knowing the object of his travel, because he suddenly did not want to return to the empty house, or to the hospital, to radiant Billie and the parade of friends who came devotedly to visit her every day of her confinement, and of course, after the birth, the professors from her department and those bleeding-heart doctoral students, who could shed with suspicious ease their vocal consciences and declare to him privately—a chummy hand on his shoulder—that they also think people with tendencies to violence have to be dealt with sternly, concluding with a sort of co-conspiratorial smile of distaste, saying that they can imagine how hard it is to work there, in the dark, with those animals who would sell their mothers for a penny and who will stab anyone who turns his back to them, and he would smile at them, for Billie, and while doing so look into them. It was actually during the last few weeks that he began seeing them for what they were, and wondering which one of them would be the first to break down in a third-degree interrogation, and who would sneak of his own accord into his office to inform on his best friend, and which of them would turn in his parents in order to gain a favor. No, he decided that he did not want to go back there just now, home, or to Israel at all: he deserved a rest, too. He had gone through several difficult weeks, yes—and he turned the truck off the road and stopped and smoked a cigarette. Afterwards, he walked into the field, stepping between the thistles and smelling them, drawing stalks of grass through his fingers, sucking his cheeks in. He meditated on the locals (as he called them) he had seen that morning, and on Billie's friends—he himself had no friends other than her—and pictured them one after another on the background of the disk of the fierce sun, saw how they became completely transparent, so that you could see the simple gears of their insincerity and their fears and mostly—and this was most surprising of all—their insignificance.

Gidi sat, leaning against the trunk of an olive tree, thinking in a monotone: I have a son, I have a son. He felt that he had to shout it, in Arabic, and he slowly turned his head toward the tree and pressed his face into a wide and pleasant hollow in its trunk. It was dim and full of a far-off fragrance that he loved. Gidi wondered who was guilty, he or other people, in that he could no longer believe in anybody, or in anything visible, or in the simple emotions which had become in his trained hands handles to be pulled and pushed.

Then he thought that he did not want to be there, in the twilight area created when two peoples turn their dark, corrupt sides toward each other, and the thought startled him, because he loved his work and believed in it, and felt that it gave him the necessary rules with which to navigate through his life. But he also knew clearly that when two apples touch one another at a single point of decay, the mold spreads over both of them.

He hunched his shoulders, curled up tightly, and lay that way for a few minutes. Then he rose and returned to the truck, guiding himself heavily and knowing that he felt very bitter, and something in his eyes clouded everything, even in the fierce light.

12

Sumud

"A year has passed since I stopped writing . . . I have overcome my despair, as other people have overcome their despair, and I emerged from it wiser, perhaps, but certainly more adamant in my decision to maintain my *sumud*, just as the Israeli government seems more determined than ever to empty the West Bank of us, the *samadin*. I now feel, more than my immediate personal fears, an objective fear of the tragedy awaiting all of us. I am now once more able to see what vanished last year—the individual faces on the wheel of death, Palestinian and Israeli faces, all struggling to halt its progress."

So wrote Raj'a Shehade, lawyer and author, in the epilogue to his book *The Third Way*.

Sumud means to endure. To stick to one's guns. To remain firmly planted on one's land. The term was coined at the Baghdad summit of Arab states in 1978 (*samadin*—the endurers) as a name for the million and a half Palestinian refugees who live under the Israeli occupation. The summit established the Steadfastness Aid Fund, meant to direct $150 million a year to these Palestinians—including those who have lived under Israeli rule since 1948—but this has become but a trickle in recent years, because Arab countries have not met their commitments to the fund.

Five years have passed since Shehade wrote those words. When you are not a free man, time passes more slowly: your soul is delayed and defeated along the way. You unconsciously moderate your actions and responses in order to be prepared for any evil. Any unexpected capriciousness of the occupier. Or of the situation itself. The time which passes for the inhabitants of the West Bank and Gaza under Israeli rule cannot even be measured in prison terms. Its end is unknown, and this makes it even harder to deal with. I asked Shehade if he had not tired at the end of these five years, at the end of twenty years, of being *sumud*.

"No," he said, "I go on believing in it. Of the two ways open to me as a Palestinian—to surrender to the occupation and collaborate with it, or to take up arms against it, two possibilities which mean, to my mind, losing one's humanity—I choose the third way. To remain here. To see how my home becomes my prison, which I do not want to leave, because the jailer will then not allow me to return."

Sumud expresses tenacity and stamina, and a sort of passive combativeness, gritting one's teeth to keep from giving in, and to keep from losing one's mind. *Sumud* means to bow one's head and live, somehow, until the storm passes. Shehade is consciously *sumud*—and was even before the Baghdad summit labeled him as such.

Other Palestinians are almost unconscious *samadin*, practically turning their expert passivity into an art.

I tell Shehade that there are such *samadin* among the Israelis as well: many people who do not accept the situation but who do not know what to do about it. They cling to the desire to remain ignorant and unaware. Faithful to their half-closed consciousness, they immerse themselves in a despairing, miserable moral slumber: "Wake me when it's over."

And what does the occupation do to us, the Israelis, in your opinion?

"I think about that a lot," Shehade answers (our conversation was conducted in English). "First, you must remember that it is not just an occupation. From a legal point of view it is an occupation, but it is actually much worse than an occupation: after all, you do not work among us just to prevent violent attacks upon yourselves. You have taken other, exceptional steps, such as establishing settlements. Nor do the civil administration and the military government work for the benefit of the local population, as they like to say they do. The military government itself is confused. The people there will tell you how much they have improved our lives. They won't tell you about the twelve hundred amendments and new laws they promulgated in the West Bank. Those are laws meant to make the current situation permanent, gradually but irrevocably. The occupation is selfish. It only acts in matters which affect it directly. Security matters are seen to with great care, but the police station in Ramallah has no sign that says "Police" in Arabic. Only in Hebrew and English. The Israeli policemen don't even pretend that they are there to protect the locals. West

Bank crime is growing and becoming more serious, but Israel is doing nothing to prevent it. It doesn't affect the occupation.

"What happened to you is what Professor Yeshayahu Leibowitz predicted immediately after the '67 war. He said then that it is impossible to be occupiers and remain moral. Even people with moral intentions are led slowly into an immoral situation. The situation turns into a sort of monster with a life of its own, which can no longer be controlled. An unjust and immoral monster. You have two kinds of people in Israel. One is the kind you called 'the *samadin* of ignorance.' They simply disconnect themselves from what is going on. The second kind uses every means to achieve its goal. The first kind of people say: An honest, sensitive man of conscience like Efraim Sneh [until recently head of the civil administration] should not do the work of the establishment. They want to cut the Arabs off from all the positive forces in Israel. Afterwards, you can't understand why the Arabs are so wild and violent. You see, you can't treat people in a certain way for years and not expect that they will react to it, right?"

Israelis sometimes ask the mirror image of that question: Why is it so easy to control you? How can you explain the fact that we rule more than a million and a half Arabs, almost without feeling it? After all, were the situation reversed, wouldn't we make your lives miserable?

Shehade smiles sadly. He is a small man, of delicate appearance, and projects a strong presence. And exactly because he is so fragile, it is clear from the start that it is hard to frighten him with any sort of physical threat: he has already come to terms with that, as it were, and the discussion passes on to other, deeper subjects, where he is very sure of himself. In his book he writes: "How easy it certainly is for the Israelis. It takes no effort to rule a society accustomed to paternalism to the point that people do not even ask who is giving the orders. We make use of and accept authority so naturally that we do not even see the humiliation and shame it engenders. The Israelis need only glide down the path prepared for them and rake in all the profits."

He tells me of the Jordanian occupation. Those are his words: the occupation. Of the intentional Jordanian effort to rewrite Palestinian history and obliterate Palestinian identity. Of the breaking of the Palestinians and the destruction of their society. "Imagine it—when King Hussein would come to Ramallah, we were all required to go out and stand along the roads, waiting for him for hours—he never came on time—and applaud when he arrived. Yes, there was oppression then, and today, too. You see, I am becoming an expert on oppression. You ask why it is easy to rule us? Check out how many people have been exiled. Many thousands of people have been exiled [more than two thousand have been expelled from the area since 1967, according to data collected by Dr. Meron Benvenisti—DG]. Whenever someone has expressed an opinion about anything, he has found himself on the other side of the bridge. Today there are far fewer expulsions, because there is no one left to exile. You have not allowed any leadership of any kind to remain here. You have ripped our society apart."

In any case, what do you do with your emotions about the occupation? How do you take out such constant frustration?

"I write. I work against injustices inflicted on Pales-

tinians by the administration. I established the Law in
the Service of Man organization. I do things so as not
to fall silent. Whom do I hate? I am filled with repulsion
when I meet some of the fools who manage our affairs.
It is not hate but pity. There was a case in the military
court—I generally prefer not to represent clients there,
it is too emotional a matter for me—when I told myself:
Take it easy, don't get excited. But I could not help it.
I boiled over. The Israelis there were so rude and unfeeling! That is, they were rude, noisy, vulgar, and un-
cultured, just as they are everywhere. I asked the sec-
retary there, a nice girl, not all there, and not herself
responsible for anything (that's what I thought then, but
today I think that there is no such thing as not being
responsible; everyone is responsible), I asked her why I
had to leave all my human qualities behind me at the
door when I entered your building. And she said blandly,
What are you talking about? It didn't matter to her! I
stood there and vented my anger, in an unfeeling world
that neither paid attention to it nor understood it! What
kind of life do your people have, your people who manage our lives? That girl, still so young, and she has to
work in something that has no connection with what is
real, only with the oppression and humiliation and the
violation of the natural rights of every man! And there
are thousands like her! After all, all your young people
pass through these territories!

"Or another instance: The authorities were going to
destroy a house in the neighborhood where I grew up.
A house full of memories and emotions for me. I stood
there and I saw how the soldiers measured the thickness
of the walls in order to decide where to lay the explosives. They did it with such matter-of-factness! We stood

there, I and the owner of the house, and we saw how they measured, and it was horrible. It was like seeing someone measure a live person for a coffin. I looked at the soldiers. So young! It is a challenge for me: to understand how they can do it. One of the answers is that they are racists. They simply don't see the family that lives in that house as their brothers, human beings."

Have you ever tried to put yourself in their place? How would you act if you were in a similar situation?

"I certainly understand the dilemma Israelis find themselves in. I don't mean to imply that Arabs are angels. Not at all. I understand the importance of military service for Israelis. But if you serve in the army you support something that is out of your control. On the other hand, as an Israeli you cannot decide to serve and yet not to serve. I think that, were I Israeli, I would devote the same energy I devote to military service to attempts to make peace. That would, perhaps, be one way to deal with the contradiction."

I asked him what he feels with regard to the settlers. Here, for the first time, Shehade lost his keen sense of humor and abandoned the low voice he had used until now.

"In my eyes they are criminals. Criminals and lunatics. Sometimes I have to meet them. They are racists. Look, racism is hard to diagnose precisely. There are many things that seem to be racism but are not. Real racism is when you don't see another person as human. They ask—with deep inner conviction—why the Arabs don't accept what they want to do here? They don't understand that, as human beings, the Arabs desire everything that any human being desires. They simply are not willing to understand that!"

And after so many years of contact and mutual acquaintance, don't you see something positive in Israel's effect on the Arabs?

"At the beginning I believed that the Israelis really were a sort of new race. And there really are some good things about you: friendship, frankness, the strong feeling of mutual responsibility. That impressed me. You definitely have created something new in liberating yourself from the past and attempting to create a new life for yourselves. The problem is that when it clashes with my freedom, in the West Bank, it is a little difficult for me to be enthusiastic about it. Israel is, in a way, a positive challenge for the Arabs. It has momentum. It is the resuscitation of something that was almost dead. It is hard to come to any clear conclusion about this, because, in comparison with the Jews in Israel, the Jews in the world at large have progressed much more intellectually, culturally, and even economically. Your legal system is impressive. Of course, it is regressing as a result of the occupation. That corrupts everything. The occupation continually presents strange, twisted challenges that it is hard for a system of justice to provide answers to. The truth is that you suffer greatly from the occupation. Britain conquered half the world, but it was then a mature nation, prepared for it. Israel was not prepared. You were too young."

Have you met Arabs who have adopted or who imitate—as a method of assimilation—Israeli modes of behavior?

"There are people like that here and there. Mostly those who work with the authorities. I once met, in the context of my work as an attorney, an Arab whose job was to interrogate security detainees. He sported a pistol on his belt. His work is hard, you know—there are prisoners who are very hard to break. Sometimes he has to beat them. Sometimes even his Israeli commander has to chew him out for that—really. His life is much easier under the occupation. They also taught him to shoot. But there aren't many like him. And I have more proof that, for you, the occupation is not successful, and that we have not surrendered completely. You would think that, if the Hebrew language is part of a higher culture, it would be a strong influence on Arabic, right? But the only Hebrew words which have been absorbed into Palestinian Arabic are 'roadblock,' 'traffic light,' and, oh, right—'walkie-talkie.' And what has happened to Hebrew during the same period?"

I tried to remember. A large number of Arabic words had been naturalized by Hebrew even before '67, probably as a result of our acquaintance with another group of Arabs, those who live in and are citizens of Israel. But today you hear many more Arabic words in daily conversation, in all different contexts. Raj'a Shehade, Christian, thirty-five years old, single. Son to one of the families of the Arab aristocracy. His father, also a lawyer, was murdered, apparently by Palestinian extremists, and the murderers have yet to be found. Raj'a Shehade himself has many connections in the United States and in Europe, and he has many Israeli friends. In the twilight region between the conqueror and the conquered, Shehade stands out as a man sensitive to nuances; he seems to me to be one for whom the blind, anonymous occupation threatens his personal sense of individualism, rather than his Arab or national identity. For this reason, perhaps, he keeps his head above water, exposing himself (sometimes dangerously) to critical Israeli eyes, challenging Arab society as well, confirming again and again his uniqueness, his existence.

I asked him how he feels when he leaves Israel for another country.

"That experience, of foreign travel, is very important to me, for the very reason that Israel continually claims that it is a part of Western culture. You should understand: the Israelis are not satisfied with having conquered us. They want to turn us into a colony of theirs, in every sense of the word, culturally as well. That means that they don't want only to confiscate land, but also to impose themselves on the soul and thoughts of the conquered. It is very important for Israelis—in a sometimes touching way—to impress us. To convince us how much Israel is superior to us. And by the way, there is a huge difference between the propaganda that Israel directs toward the West Bank, where it wants to appear omnipotent, and the propaganda it directs toward the West, in whose eyes it wants to appear as a victim, surrounded by powerful enemies.

"Overseas travel was important for me, because I had become accustomed to your occupation. I had become accustomed to Israeli rudeness, cynicism, idiocy, and arrogance, and it was very important for me to see whether that was the only true reality. A person begins to forget things after a few years. Is that the price that people must pay for the progress they have achieved? Must they become rude technocrats, suppressing values they have buried deep inside them, lacking sensitivity to human emotions and suffering? So every time I leave the country I look for alternatives. I look for standards by which I can correctly evaluate our situation here, and reconfirm to myself that it is not inevitable, that what I see here is a counterfeit of the truth. It gives me more strength to face reality. And when Israel tried to impose its patterns of thinking and behavior, and tell me that it is the best, I can respond to that challenge and prove that other nations have done it differently. That it's possible to have a national consciousness, as the English and the French and the Americans do, and remain yourselves, and not lose the most positive human elements that you have. There are peoples with strong feelings of national pride who, despite that, are completely different. That encourages me and shows me that in the future the Palestinians can have an independent and proud nationalism, and behave completely differently from the way you present yourselves. For that reason, whenever I left the country and was asked about my destination at the airport, I answered: 'Civilization.' Here there is no civilization. You try to impress us—and yourselves. You say: We have highways and fighter planes and tanks that we made ourselves, we are liberated people, and you Arabs are primitive; and I had to leave here to discover that it's not true."

You certainly know that there are many Israelis who argue that "time is with us." In your opinion, is the fact that the political situation with regard to the territories has been frozen for so long to Israel's benefit?

"It seems to me that the long term is more dangerous for Israel than for us. The Arab world is now in a miserable state, there is no denying that. It is a world that is bad to live in. A world of oppression. But Israel is founded on so many contradictions, and on so many opposing forces, that its existence is always in great danger. For example, there is a huge gap between the self-image of Israelis and reality. You think you are omnipotent, because of your success in controlling such a large Arab population. But the truth is that foreign support is the decisive factor. You remind me of the spoiled son of a rich man, who thinks he can do anything, until he has to face life on his own and discovers a few hard truths.

"Another thing: you are still misled by your belief that millions of Jews will still come here. That, after all, is one of the important arguments you have for settling the West Bank! But the Jews of the Diaspora have no intention of coming here. They have a good life where they are!

"And you have another mistaken assumption: you think that Israel will be strong forever, and will get out of the present situation in one piece. You prefer to forget that the Arabs are developing. Part of that is to your credit, of course. We are now more exposed to the world. There are many foreign visitors. We are not standing still. You, however, are stuck. You are prisoners of your conceptions and refuse to recognize reality. It seems to me that to live in an area full of hostility and think that you can do so forever, without making any effort to come to terms with your neighbors, is simply not rational. You display no creative thinking about how to solve the conflict. You . . ."

Excuse me for interrupting, but do you hear creative thinking of that sort from Arabs?

"For now, we are not in a position to propose attractive or inspired things. We can only respond to proposals that reconfirm our humanity and our personal and national pride. That, unfortunately, is the state we are in. We can only respond to proposals, and they don't arrive. The Likud voices its opinions. They are not, in my opinion, correct, but they express them clearly and influence the public. The Labor Party plays a cynical game. It could have certain political effects, of course, but it contains nothing new or earthshaking that could bring about any real change or solution to the problem. Look at the blindness of Ber Borochov [the early Zionist who inspired the fathers of today's Labor Zionists], who wrote in 1900, in Russian: 'They [the Palestinians] have no reason to greet us with unfriendliness. On the contrary: they believe that the land is justly that of the Jews.' That blindness continues today in the supposedly enlightened Labor Party, which still believes it deep inside. And now, if all these mistaken assumptions determine your policy, consciously or unconsciously, how can your policy be successful?"

I still cannot understand how Shehade does not tire of and despair from his *sumud*.

"I do not despair. I only fear for the future. The occupation is steadily destroying us. It destroys the entire fabric of civil and traditional life. We are caught in a totally false reality, and are beginning to think that it is the truth. That is a great danger. But I do not despair: there are so many things to fight for. There are so many things to improve! From looking after mental-health institutions to the effort to set up a law school. There is not a single law school in the entire West Bank. There are a million things that a person can devote himself to. You can't give up. Independence, for me, is not only a piece of paper or a declaration. You have to work hard to achieve it, and it is possible to do so much even now."

Later, Raj'a Shehade said: "One of the things which, for me, gives meaning to my life is that the situation is a challenge: to remain human even under the conditions that prevail. To answer honestly the questions that the situation presents. Questions that a normal person can live his entire life without needing to deal with. Not to surrender to despair. Not to allow myself to give in and become a hater. People who speak a language of violence speak a very tempting language. And when I say violence I don't mean only physical, concrete action. There is also quieter, camouflaged violence. Sometimes I feel that I would very much want to take on that language for myself. I have to fight against that constantly. I am always on guard."

The Censor

In a chance conversation with two Arab intellectuals—the poet and critic Muhammed Albatrawi, and the author 'Ali Alkhalili—both made reference to the military censorship of their writings.

Albatrawi: "Every word of mine goes through the censorship office. In my poems, I am forbidden to write Yafa, *the Arabic name for the city Jaffa, and must use the Hebrew form* Yafo. *I can't write* 'Askalan *and must write* Ashkelon. *Instead of* Falastin, Palestine, *I write 'my land.' Sometimes I write a simple love song and the great Israeli censor decides it is a nationalist Palestinian poem. For this reason I try to write with great clarity, so that they won't mistakenly ascribe to me other intentions and red-pencil whole lines and verses. It goes without saying that this affects the work's literary value. I have to guess and take into account what the Israeli censor will think, and refrain from getting him angry at me. You have to remember that there are more than two thousand books banned in the West Bank. Some of them are works of Israeli Arab writers, which we are forbidden to read in the West Bank, poets like Samih Alqassem and Tawfiq Zayyad. I can never know in advance how the censor will react: sometimes I write something risky and he approves it without a comment, and sometimes I write something totally innocent and it is banned completely. It can drive you crazy, because there is no logic to it.*

"I've often wondered who the man is, how he can shred my thoughts with a wave of his scissors. I sometimes try to guess who he is by the way he crosses things out: sometimes I think he must be a recent graduate of the Arabic department at the university who feels some holy and juvenile calling to wipe out every threat, even the imaginary ones. There are censors who, I sense, are pedantic bureaucrats, because they consistently cross out only certain words, no matter what the context is. I think the censor must be a very frightened man, bored with his work, maybe even ashamed of it: after all, it is so much easier to cross out a verse than to delve into it and try to grapple with what it means."

Alkhalili: "If you don't want all the copies of your book to be confiscated immediately upon publication, you must send the manuscript to the censor. I think it is horrible, because a writer needs to act with complete freedom. What happens to me now, after twenty years of battles and censorship of my work, is that I find myself, to my horror, developing a little Israeli censor inside me, who keeps an eye on me. It has suddenly become clear to me that in a way I am no longer a free man.

"I spend a lot of time thinking about my Israeli censor:
he must be some low-level clerk who wants to do his
work without getting into trouble with his superiors.
That is why, when he has any doubts, he prefers to
delete. Sometimes I can feel how angry he is at me by
how deep his pen has gouged the manuscript. I don't
think he really likes his job. Somewhere inside, he certainly must feel that he is like an executioner. Words,
after all, are things full of life, of humanity, and his job
is to cut their heads off.

"Once I carried on an indirect dialogue with the censor. I wrote, for a newspaper, a story about Juha, the
great fool of Arab folktales, and the censor banned it.
Then I wrote another story about 'the man who does
not laugh.' I portrayed him as a bitter man, ugly inside
and out, who sits in a dark corner and hates everyone,
himself included. The censor approved the story without
any deletions, and added a note in his own handwriting:
'But I like stories about Juha.' "

13

A Doll at

the Allenby Bridge

"My cousin from Amman came to visit me for my birthday," Raj'a Shehade tells in his book *The Third Way*. "He cursed me for two days after his arrival, and accused me of being responsible for everything that happened to him at the Allenby Bridge when he came from Jordan. The cries of the children when he was stripped for a body search; the sight of a corpse, in transfer for burial in the West Bank, taken out of its coffin for a security search; the stink of the feet of travelers after hours of waiting for their shoes, which had been sent for X-ray examination; the heartrending wails of a mother whose fourteen-year-old son had been taken for interrogation and had not yet been returned. All this, and the long hours that each person waits for his name to be called."

I must go see for myself. Is it as he says it is?

A hot wind blows north from Arabia. Far off, Jericho shimmers behind a veil of dust circling lazily over the bottom of the world and of memory: Jericho. Along the way there, the absurd refugee camps, ruins of ruins, with a bicycle path alongside the road, as in Europe, and young people walk along it reciting their lessons, not because they like studying outside that much, but because it is too crowded at home. An energetic boy sails on his bike, carrying behind him a box containing a few chicks, some of them already dying in the heat.

Closer up, it is a different Jericho, a shady, slightly unruly resort city set out around its squares and the whispers of its springs and trees and the red splashes of the bougainvillea and the scandalous summerhouses of the West Bank wealthy. Capricious Jericho.

I stop briefly to talk with the Governor of Jericho ("A governor must be a father to the inhabitants," he says with much self-importance) and continue on by way of the plain, choking under the layers of dusty air, past the banana and date groves and the abandoned monasteries, and arrive at the Allenby Bridge.

There is nothing like the open bridges between the West Bank and Jordan for illustrating Israeli policy with regard to the territories. When then Minister of Defense Moshe Dayan decided after the war in 1967 to allow people and merchandise to pass over the bridges, he wanted to break down psychological barriers, create the possibility for Jews and Arabs to become acquainted with each other, and create tight economic dependence and a sort of de facto coexistence. The open-bridges policy was also meant to demonstrate that Israel allows freedom of access to holy sites in Jerusalem and freedom of worship to all religions. Another goal which guided Dayan, also very important, was to turn the open bridges into a safety valve for releasing the excess tension that he expected would build up among the West Bankers as a result of the occupation. The knowledge that it is possible "to go out and get some air," to enter, for a time, the Arab world, to study there, to do business there, to visit relatives, has a huge influence on the people of the West Bank and Gaza Strip.

The bottom line of Israeli policy in the conquered territories, says Shlomo Gazit, Israel's first Coordinator of Activities in the territories, in his book *The Carrot and the Stick*, has been to create a situation in which "they have something to lose." And in fact, Israel's ability to close and open the bridges has become a powerful tool in its hands, and the most important of its deterrents. There have been cases in which the travelers crossing the bridge have jeered the inhabitants of Nablus or Ramallah who arrived at the bridge only to find their crossing prohibited because of some crime which took place in one of those cities, while the bridge remained open for all others.

On the other hand, Gazit notes, the open-bridges policy has, paradoxically, been an obstacle to progress toward a comprehensive political solution. This great pressure valve has made it easier for Israel to control the territories, and in doing so has dulled the urgent need to find a long-range political solution. Dr. Meron Benvenisti told me that the open-bridges policy is an efficient weapon for Jordan as well, in its efforts to impose its will on the West Bankers: when the director of the East Jerusalem Chamber of Commerce, Fa'ik Barakat (the man responsible for granting passage certificates for the bridges), once made an anti-Jordanian comment on the radio, he discovered upon arriving at the bridge that Amman had forwarded instructions not to grant him an entrance permit. Jordan and Israel apply such pressure on entire villages, if one of the two countries discerns irregular activity in them. This quiet "war" can take on even more critical forms: Israel, in its desire to encourage the emigration of young Arabs, decreed that West Bank residents between the ages of twenty and thirty cannot return home within nine months of their exit from the West Bank. Jordan responded to this with a measure of its own, forbidding (between 1980 and 1982) that such young people reside in its territory for more than a month. In these power struggles it is the Palestinians who suffer, of course—"asses that anyone can ride," in the words of Taher, the man from the village near Hebron.

At the entrance to the waiting area by the bridge sprawl a group of Israeli soldiers, reservists. I had already noticed that the reservists who police the West Bank have a special expression and build: something which projects an unconscious detachment of the man from himself. Reservists are always good at suppressing their individuality, but in the West Bank they become exceptionally talented at it.

A surprising silence reigns in the waiting area. The dozens of Arabs waiting their turn to be examined by the soldiers sit motionless on the plastic benches, and bide their time until their name is trumpeted over the loudspeaker. When your name is called, you must get up, approach the soldier holding your belongings, and answer questions while he examines them. The soldier empties the suitcases on the counter, fingers everything, confiscates anything with writing on it (including plastic bags with store logos and T-shirts), forbids the entry of all electrical appliances, wooden items, and cosmetics—in short, anything which might conceivably be a security threat or which might contain explosives. Toys must be confiscated, because they have in the past served as containers for detonators. That is the reason why you often hear the bitter crying of children here. Afterwards, your shoes are sent to be X-rayed, and you yourself enter a small cell for a body check. A woman soldier performs the examination on women and children. Even the baby's disposable diaper must be removed, because not long ago a young woman was caught trying to smuggle explosives in one of those all-absorbent Pampers.

I have come on an easy day. Relatively few visitors. Everyone breathes freely today, and the examinations go quickly. It takes only three hours from the moment you arrive from Jordan until your exit from the waiting room. But it is not always like this: an average of 400,000 people cross the bridges every year. During the summer visiting months, the place is intolerable: flies fill the air, the heat is oppressive, children scream, and people are stuck here for many long hours. Sometimes as long as ten hours of such waiting.

The reservist serving as a bag searcher at the bridge relates: "On a busy day you cannot be judicious and polite. I've seen soldiers who throw out clothes and belongings of Arabs out of spite and in order to hurt them. More than once I've seen a young, angry soldier use his position to humiliate an elderly and venerable man, making him run all over the place in his socks, jeer and degrade him in front of people from his village. You can only guess what that man feels about Israel after such treatment."

The shoes of the travelers return in a single crate, which the travelers then storm. You can often see an Arab, by his dress penniless and poverty-stricken, worm his way out of the mob, shiny patent-leather shoes in his hands, while a wealthy-looking lawyer is left disappointedly holding a pair of battered sandals from the bottom of the crate.

Porters and janitors, Arabs from Jericho who undergo a security examination at the hands of the soldiers when they arrive every morning, also work in the waiting area. The reservist with whom I spoke said, "An odd system of masters and slaves is developing with these Arabs. They work with us—but they are always suspect. It is an unclear and unpleasant situation."

One can see the authorities' efforts to make it easier for the incoming travelers at the bridge. The reserve units sent to serve there are made up of top-flight soldiers, there is air conditioning (but in the summer you would not know it), and recently five young stewardesses from Jericho have been added to the staff, their job being to mediate between the perplexed civilian and the authorities in charge of the passage point, and to explain to him what the process is and what he is expected to do.

There can be no doubt that, under present conditions, the discomfort suffered by the travelers over the bridge is unavoidable. That is, as long as Israel oversees the passage of Palestinians from Jordan to the West Bank. The damage done to Israel here is, however, very great. Even on an easy day such as the day I visited, I could feel immediately how this place becomes a hothouse for the growth of enmity toward Israel; how, as a result of the unpleasant friction between civilians and soldiers, the hate always lying in wait under a thin cover of surrender and silence is quickly bared. Today the travelers over the bridge accept this right as self-evident. They are not aware of all the political considerations behind it. They know only that an Israeli soldier fingers their personal belongings, the hair on their heads and in their groins; that he makes their old mothers wait five hours in the heat to be examined; that he steals their children's teddy bears. Any one of us who has had a similar experience—even if immeasurably milder—in any European airport, and anyone who has had any personal belonging of his confiscated for ten minutes—certainly knows the feeling of rage and insult that came over him, and how easy it is to judge, bitterly and without distinction, the entire country at the gates of which it happened.

"Once," the reservist went on to tell me, "one traveler under examination thanked me, in English, for having refolded his clothes, which had been disturbed during the examination. He was very surprised by that—he had never encountered such treatment. Another time a woman came to me with a three-year-old girl. The girl held a plastic doll, and according to orders toys are to be confiscated. Since it was a quiet, unpressured day, I decided to take the doll apart, in order to make sure that it was 'clean,' and to allow the girl to take it with her. I carefully took apart the mechanism that says 'Mama,' the hands and the feet, the stomach and the head. The soldiers around me made fun of me. They called me a 'peacenik.' There was nothing in the doll. I put the doll back together and I was about to give it back to the girl. Then the bridge commander came and told me to confiscate it. I explained that the doll was no danger. He insisted. The girl cried horribly, and her mother pleaded tearfully. The commander said: 'We cannot make exceptions.' The doll was confiscated."

The Arabs themselves display no emotion. From the minute they disembark from the buses which bring them from their visit in Jordan, they place an impenetrable mask on their faces. I saw them as they came. Their expressions reminded me of what I used to feel when I came back to basic training after a short furlough. Even during the examination, they do not change their expression. The children learn to put on that expression from a very young age when faced with a soldier. Sometimes, at the end of the procedure, you can see a quick glance of hate or pain, or a calming hug—so tight as to hurt—that a father gives to the crying son on his shoulder. Something is recorded somewhere in their memory.

Later, on my way to the bridge, I passed the great red bridge trucks. Merchandise can be transferred from Israel to Jordan only in these trucks. They are special trucks, most of their parts visible to the examining eye. Every part of the truck has a special seal, the absence of which immediately alerts the examiner that a change has been made in the vehicle. On every such truck, there are hundreds of such seals. A transparent window has been added to the gas tanks, in order to allow examination of the contents of the tank. They have thought of everything here, but even so, terrorists manage to smuggle weapons into the area from time to time. The war continues.

And at the end—the bridge itself, over the Jordan flowing lazy and brown, running around the clumps of reeds. An Israeli position opposite a Jordanian position. Two machine guns yawning at each other. Jordanian soldiers in blue uniforms and blue berets stare at me from behind torn sandbags. Once each day, the commanders of the bridge from both sides meet exactly halfway across, in order to make necessary technical arrangements. Each day, they trade newspapers. I stride to the middle of the bridge and halt. The border and the river awaken strange and unexpected urges in me. Then I return.

I went to the bridges mostly because of the harsh section from Shehade's book. And because of another story told me by the reservist, who has known Shehade well for several years:

"One of the things that was like a nightmare for me was the fear that I would meet Raj'a Shehade at the bridge. And then, one day, in the early afternoon, I raised my head and I saw Raj'a. He came with a small parcel. I asked the soldier examining him to let me take care of him. Raj'a was returning from the United States by way of Amman. The major part of the material he had with him was posters from the New York exhibition of paintings from the Hermitage Museum in Leningrad. He had some clothes as well. It was an indescribably awkward meeting. We both said something like 'What a place to meet . . .' I could, actually, have avoided examining him, but I remembered the passages he wrote in his book about going over the bridge, and I wanted to save him one time from that experience. At least once."

14

The Wastonaires

An unofficial public institution functioning alongside the Israeli military government and civil administration, the "wastonaires" are a product of the occupation. In the local slang, *wasta* means "mediation." So the wastonaire is an intermediary—or, in other contexts, a pimp. In the special context of the West Bank this is not, however, just the name of a profession.

The wastonaires are usually from the middle or lower classes, some of them former criminals who have come up in the world and won wealth and power by grace of a sharp and no-nonsense instinct for spotting the opportunities presented by the existing complex and murky situation. Most of them began as collaborators with the security forces, and then, when their relations with the military government had become well established, they began to present themselves to the populace as possessing contacts and influence within the administration. There were men of similarly sharp and quick instincts in the military government who immediately understood that it was worthwhile fostering such contacts and helping the collaborators refurbish their image.

So, when a local Arab presents a request to the administration—for a building permit, for example—and his request is rejected, justly or unjustly, he now has the recourse of turning to the man with the connections, the wastonaire, who has the run of the corridors of the military government headquarters. These intermediaries have become the representatives of the populace, which has no choice but to make use of them, galling as it is. The wastonaire approaches "his man" in the military government and presents his clients' petitions. The military government official, interested in furthering the reputation of the wastonaire in the eyes of the locals, frequently approves the requests. In exchange for this, the wastonaire is expected both to provide the military government with information and gossip and to influence and direct those with whom he comes in contact. It is not hard to imagine how this process is managed, what it has achieved, and what things are understood but never spoken.

Since, for all intents and purposes, every request for a permit by a local resident must be approved by the military—meaning that the military can deny it, even unjustly and with intentional arbitrariness—the locals must frequently apply to the military government through the wastonaires. Villagers from the Hebron area quoted me the following prices:

Arranging a building permit: 250–300 Jordanian dinars ($750–$900)

Arranging a business permit: 500–1,000 Jordanian dinars ($1,500–$3,000)

Arranging family reunification (the most coveted of permits): 3,000 Jordanian dinars ($9,000).

A terrorist cell was uncovered some years ago in a certain village, and a curfew was imposed for an unlimited period of time. For the village farmers, forbidden to go out to their fields, this meant in essence the loss of an entire year's crops. The villagers were powerless to do anything. The wastonaire in this particular place was the village elder, the mukhtar (a not uncommon combination). He demanded a thousand dinars from each family in order to arrange for the curfew to be lifted. Those with money paid and were allowed to leave the village immediately. Those without money remained restricted to the village for four entire weeks, and their crops withered.

These are extreme examples, but it is the common, everyday cases which are most infuriating. Generally, the unholy alliance between the regime and its agents means that Arabs are forced to pay large sums of money in order to receive what is, though they may not know it, theirs by right and according to law. The attitude of the locals to the wastonaires is mixed: they despise them, but they need them; they curse them, but are afraid to cross them.

I brought the subject up in conversations with officials in the civil adminstration. This was their comment:

"As to the wastonaire phenomenon—there is a lot of exaggeration. There are not many people who take bribes in order to arrange people's rights for them." As a matter of fact, one may assume that the wastonaires, gentle souls, will use any means to ensure that they remain a scarce commodity. The same "high-placed official" went on to say: "You have to understand that we are speaking here of a population not yet free of the customs of the Arab world. It is only natural for the civil administration to encourage people who contribute through their activity and influence to the community, in the sense of keeping things calm, which allows the economy to flourish and is therefore for the general good."

I appreciated his frankness.

Not long after that conversation, I saw an Arab in civilian clothes walking through Nablus with an impressive pistol prominently displayed on his waist. I asked a local who it was, and after some hesitation, he explained to me that this was a wastonaire. I went to the civil administration and asked if it supplies such people with arms. They said: "A permit to carry a weapon is granted only in the case where a person's life is in danger, and according to certain criteria which cannot be revealed. In any case, only a few dozen people have been given weapons."

The emergence of the wastonaires is not the only phenomenon to puncture the fabric of traditional local life: the status of the mukhtar has also greatly deteriorated as a result of Israeli rule. The security forces discovered that it is easier and more convenient to approach the local mukhtar with any local problem, and demand information and cooperation from him. The few mukhtars who refused to cooperate were cleverly dealt with by means of anonymous innuendo and humiliation, after which they could no longer function in their traditional role. Today the security forces use the mukhtars to guide them to the houses of terrorist suspects. Anyone who has served in the reserves in the territories knows that when he needs to carry out a midnight search in a given house in a crowded village, or in the heart of a refugee camp, the easiest way to do so is to go to the mukhtar's house, awaken him, and order him to lead the troops to the suspect's house. In this way the security forces have turned the mukhtars into collaborators. Anyone who chances into the office of one of the military governors on a day of a meeting with the mukhtars would think that he had barged unsuspecting into a strange meeting of a quaintly dressed board of directors of a large company. The atmosphere is one of calm, coffee, gossip, and flattering laughter. The mukhtars accept with suspect naturalness the fatherlike authority of the military governor. It may be that they believe that in doing so they better serve their interests and those of their villagers, or it may be their instinct for survival. In any case, one thing is clear: the institution of the mukhtar has been taken out of its natural context, and its content has been greatly distorted.

15

Like a Boy

with a Teddy Bear

"Abu Yussuf! Abu Yussuf!"

Night. Total stillness. A dog barks in one of the shut-up factories.

"Abu Yussuf!"

P., my companion this evening, stands together with me on a hot night and calls out at one of the factories in the industrial park in Holon, a suburb of Tel Aviv. Both of us feel as if someone is watching us. From in front? From behind us? From all sides, probably. Tens, maybe even hundreds of people hide out in the industrial park at night, laborers from the territories who sleep in Israel. Their presence within the Green Line is illegal, and if the police or border guards find them, they can expect imprisonment and, usually, beatings. It is for this reason that they now conceal themselves in their rooms and do not answer us.

A long time later, after heads peering out of top-floor windows had scouted us out, and after one window opened and suspicious voices wanted to know exactly who we were and what we were looking for, and after they were convinced that our intentions were good, we were allowed in. They told us they knew we weren't from the border guard because they always call either "Abdullah" or "Muhammad." A real lack of imagination.

We entered a large hall on the top floor of a large factory. I cannot give identifying details about the factory, or about the people I met, because that was a precondition of our conversation. When I quote them, they will appear only as "voices."

In the hall, divided by sheets of plywood into two spaces, are fifteen beds. It is very hot inside. The owner has given them an old fan about the size of those used in automobiles. The place is lit by a single neon lamp. Towels are hung on clotheslines which run the length of the hall. It is ten o'clock at night, and the laborers are getting ready for bed. Some wear only pants, some only underwear, because of the heat. Cigarette butts, candy wrappers, and old newspapers are strewn over the floor. They look P. and me over with exhausting suspicion. For now, they do not talk. Only their *ra'is*, the procurer who brought the workers to work in the factory, a young muscular man in an undershirt, is allowed to speak. He is responsible for them. He is the closest to the boss. He is the one who will decide how much they can criticize or speak their minds.

This silent examination of us takes almost half an hour. P., my companion, is an Israeli Arab—a self-described Marxist–Leninist who had been a laborer for many years and who now devotes his life to improving the lot of Arab workers. He tells our hosts that a new newspaper will soon appear in Israel, to be called *Iyar, May*, which will represent the workers and defend their rights. When he asks if they have never thought of organizing themselves together with other workers, those who sleep in the adjoining factories, for instance, in order to improve their situation, they smirk.

Voice: This is a prison. You say we should organize, but we are like living dead here. I work thirteen hours a day. I have two breaks, each one for half an hour. One at ten and one at two. I don't get paid for the breaks. I have to pay for food, too. The hardest part is working from two in the afternoon until eight. Your head explodes. After a day at work I don't even have the strength to think. I can't do anything but go to sleep.

Voice: I work every day from the morning until it is dark. On Friday afternoon I go out and see the sun. [Laughs.] And on Fridays, for some reason, there is always dust in the air, and no sun!

A black-and-white television sits on an iron shelf, with a distorted picture. It is hard to guess what it shows. The workers bought the television out of their own pockets, everyone chipping in. They bought an antenna as well and asked the boss to allow them to erect it on the factory roof in order to improve the quality of the picture. He refused. They sleep between piles of raw materials for the factory. Large mice run around, unafraid. The whole time we were there, we heard a constant, annoying sound; three days previously, the factory's alarm had gone out of order. Since then it has rung without stopping. Twenty-four hours a day, though the boss promised to bring someone to fix it.

Voice: I more or less live in Tel Aviv, but I haven't seen anything here except the machine in the factory. I graduated high school in Ramallah, and I have a three-month-old daughter. We named her Sabrin, which means patience. I had a son who died two days after he was born. I don't like the work. I work on a machine and it drives me crazy. Look at the clock a hundred times an hour. I go home once a week. I get there at five in the evening on Friday and go to sleep. I sleep until twelve on Saturday. Afterwards, I fix things at home and look at my daughter to see how she's grown. She still doesn't know me. It will probably take her a long time before she does. On Sunday at seven in the morning I'm already back at my machine. I don't have any choice: I support my brothers as well. I have a brother who is taking his high-school graduation exams now, and I have to keep working here.

The *ra'is* answers a question of mine: No, thank God, we're all friends here, we get along fine with each other. There aren't any problems and no tension.

Voice: My body is too busy fighting with itself to be able to fight with all the people here.

[Laughter.]

Voice: We earn about $95 a week. That's about a dollar and a quarter an hour. When we come up here in the evening we don't leave until morning. Even if we weren't afraid of the police and the border guard, I wouldn't go to a movie. How can I shell out ten dollars on a movie and a night out when I have to support my family back home? What would I tell them? That I went out to have fun?

Voice: To get a raise, I have to go to my boss and cry. Actually cry. Our boss starts sweating when we ask him for money. He doesn't pay social security on us and we don't get cost-of-living adjustments, and of course we don't get a pay slip. We are totally dependent on him. Whoever asks for too much gets kicked out. If he kicks me out, I'm done for.

The heat intensifies. Beads of sweat drip down my forehead. Clouds of dust rise from the mattresses and wool blankets at the slightest touch. In the corner of the hall is a small cell built of bare brick, in which there is a water pipe—the shower. There is no light in the shower. Pairs of underwear hang on a clothesline stretched across the room. Each worker showers once every two days, and is allowed to stay in the shower for a quarter of an hour. The kitchen is at the other end of the hall. There is a rust-eaten gas burner and a sink. The workers eat with tin implements. They buy and cook food for themselves. They had finished a standard supper just before I arrived: potatoes, lentils, onions, and tomatoes.

They sit facing me on the beds, tired, scratching themselves. A few of them look to me as if they are fourteen years old, but they insist that they are eighteen. When I ask what year they were born, they get confused and laugh. Someone is already sleeping, mouth gaping, on one bed. Yawns dance like black flames in an endless chain around the room. The younger men already stare mindlessly into space. I ask the one sitting next to me why he and his friends do not clean the place for themselves. It would be possible, after all, to improve the atmosphere a bit. He shrugs. Too tired. No one wants to. They live here for months and years. They slowly lose contact with their friends, and with themselves.

According to the data given me by David Nagar, the director of the Committee on Workers from the Territories of the Histadrut, the Israeli national labor union, some hundred thousand laborers from the territories

now work in Israel. At least half of them are not registered with the national employment service, and therefore work in Israel illegally. They are unprotected against
exploitation and injustice, and lack in effect any rights
at all. The Histadrut, Mr. Nagar says, cannot search
them out. That is the job of the police. The Histadrut
has an interest in finding such workers, he noted, because
in doing so it can protect Jewish workers from being
crowded out by cheap labor. I asked why Histadrut
representatives do not do the simple thing that I did,
and go at night to industrial parks, find the workers,
and force the factory owners to register them as the law
requires and grant them their rights. That's the job of
the police, he said.

In the meantime, the current situation continues. It
would be possible to imagine a process by which the
young man who leaves his traditional surroundings for
the big city would develop—despite the harsh living
conditions—and discover the world and himself as an
individual, but the people I saw, and no doubt tens of
thousands of others, are regressing. They have retreated
into a demeaning, degenerate, inanimate form of existence.

Written on the plywood, between the obscene drawings:

"Important event! For the first time in the history of
work, on Thursday, the last day of the week we sleep
here, the food was not exhausted, and we ate supper,
because something unexpected happened, and we received outside assistance from Brother 'Ali, who works
in Kiryat Sharett, who brought us watermelons and can-
taloupes and number-five peaches and plums."

* * *

Midnight. In a subterranean parking garage, under a well-known restaurant. Khaled and Fateh (the names have been changed at their request), nineteen years old. From Han Yunis in the Gaza Strip. They both have children. Khaled is divorced. His two daughters live with his mother, who is raising them. He and Fateh work as dishwashers.

Khaled (thick, kinky hair, talks quickly, in Hebrew, makes jokes at his own expense, nurses his cigarette in a slightly dramatic way, an entertainer looking for a chance to perform): I work here every day from 6:30 in the morning to twelve at night. [Fateh goes and brings me their punch cards, stamped by the clock.] At twelve, I finish working. Sometimes I don't see the sun for an entire day. Only when I go to throw out the garbage I can stand for a second and see that it's still there. Once every two weeks, when I have a vacation, I remember that there is a sky and wind and stars.

Fateh: If I were to go and ask for a permit to sleep in a real apartment in Israel, not here in the storeroom, your intelligence people would tell me that to get a permit I have to work as an informer for them. There are a lot of Arab criminals here, and some of them finished college! And they all take drugs. Why? Because when one of them finishes studying, the Shin Bet comes to him and says work for us, and he says no. So they begin pressuring him, and destroy him little by little. What does he have left? Drugs. He works all day like a slave, and at night, so as not to go crazy, he smokes.

Khaled: I bring up my children, and get older, and my children will also come and work for you and grow old, and their children, too. What most hurts me is that I feel as if my mind has already gone soft. I never thought

I'd end up like this. I spend my life in the *intihar* ["suicide"—their name for washing the large pots]. I have no life outside of work. Only dirty work. No one cares about my life, no one thinks that this also is a human being who wants to do something with himself.

Fateh: Our life is trash. Once a sewage pipe in the restaurant got stopped up. The boss told me to go down and open it. I told him, I can't, it disgusts me. He said, You stopped it up, and you'll open it up. I told him that I don't know how to do that sort of thing. That he should bring someone to do it. He said, You want me to bring a Jew for that? He forced me to go down there, way inside. When I came out, I was sick. I was in bed for a whole week. The boss didn't pay me for the days I was sick. Why should he pay? A week ago my leg was scalded by hot water. I worked for four hours and then the foot went. He docked me for the whole day.

Khaled: We're slowly going crazy here. We hit each other. It's from nerves. Who can we take it out on? Only on each other. And when I come home, once every two weeks, I take it out on the family, and they really don't deserve it.

Fateh: We're the lowest. Even the assistant cooks are Jews. I can't be an assistant cook? But if I ask the boss, he says, You're an Arab. You're fit for garbage and dishwashing. They won't even let me be a waiter. Only one who looks a little Jewish is allowed to work with the customers, and even he has to change his name to Moshe or Yossi. But if you look like an Arab, the Jews don't want to see you while they're eating.

Khaled: Every day I take out ten full cans of garbage and throw it in the city's bin upstairs. There is a service elevator next to the restaurant that lets you off right near the bin, but the boss won't let us use it. So I tie the cans to a rope, and the rope around my neck, and drag, and I've made up songs I sing when I drag the garbage, and when I wash dishes.

He shuts his eyes, sucks on his cigarette, and shakes his foot like a conductor tapping his stand with his wand, and warbles nasally:

"I entered a garden through the gate / The jasmine cried and the rose bowed its head / The lilies laughed and said—Here comes the poor boy / One day we will plant peaches / And one day figs / Love is only for the rich / And I am only a poor refugee . . .

"The evil man called to a noble poor man / Come, he told him, work for me. / Serve me like my servants do. / Cook, launder, clean my house. / The noble poor man said: / Better I should climb a deserted mountain, / That the owls and ravens eat me there, / Than to work for an evil and cruel man."

Khaled concludes his song. I wait for the last notes to echo in the large empty kitchen in which we sit, and I say cautiously: "But you work for him nevertheless."

And Khaled says: "Yes, what can I do."

It is already one in the morning. They do not want to go to sleep. Our interest has awakened them. They want us to stay. With sudden enthusiasm they announce that they will prepare a meal for us. They are not willing to take no for an answer. So, in the middle of the night, in a subterranean kitchen, they switch on the microwave and set us a table graced with all the delicacies of the restaurant. They pile more and more onto the table, steaks and salads and relishes and drinks, and press us to eat, and I, I must admit, dine with great enjoyment, and I feel that eating here is a way of getting back at the boss, and at the garbage heap surrounding them up to their necks.

"You aren't going to eat?"

"No"—they laugh—"we can't stand Jewish food. Mayonnaise from a bottle! Fish and eggs together! Sometimes we take things from the refrigerator and prepare them like Arabs do."

Khaled: Sometimes the boss tells us, Here is something you are allowed to eat. It's always something that's been in the refrigerator for a week, that no one else wanted.

They have worked here for two years. I ask them if they can mention something good they have learned from the Jews, something that they gained from their life in the big city.

Khaled laughs. "I've learned only one thing here—to wash dishes. And even that my mother taught me a long time ago."

We finish our absurd midnight meal. Khaled sings another song, maybe the beginnings of another blues era, the Arab Worker Blues, and before we leave brings us a little school notebook in which he writes down his thoughts. A diary. I translate a section word for word:

"Confusion, thoughts, and sorrow, and dreams and remorse. Like the life of a prisoner who has sentenced himself to life in prison, shut all his days behind bars, behind electrified doors, in solitary confinement underground. Only by his watch can he know what the time is. He does not see true light. Only neon light. Sometimes he does not know if it is day outside, or night . . ."

Last stop: the Levinsky teachers' college.

Two in the morning. By way of an unfrequented dirt path off the road to the Tel Baruch beach, near the country club at the northern entrance to Tel Aviv, we arrive at the back yard of the Levinsky teachers' college. The college is lit on all sides. There is work going on. Two boys come down to us. They do not have keys. They are shut up here each night, and in the morning someone comes to let them out. We talk to them through an iron net. They are not afraid to give their names: 'Ali and Samir from the Jabalia refugee camp in the Gaza Strip. The first is fifteen years old, and the second sixteen.

'Ali: "A cleaning contractor named Rafi brought us here. We've worked here every night for a month and a half. We come every day at six in the evening, when the Jews go, and leave at seven in the morning, before they arrive. Every night, we clean and mop all the rooms. There are maybe fifty rooms here, and we are by ourselves. Sometimes there is someone else with us, an Arab, and there is also an old guard, who is scared of everyone, including us."

Samir (dark-faced, with large eyes): "We work all week. Even on Friday nights. We get $375 a month. No pay slip. No social security. We finish work at seven in the morning, and sleep in an apartment the contractor rented for all his workers. All kinds sleep there. We buy food ourselves. Don't cook. We eat hummus and salad. We're in the apartment until the evening, and then we come back here. We mop until four in the morning, and then we are tired and go to sleep a little. We put three chairs together in the hallway and sleep on them."

I write. The fence dividing us casts a barred shadow on the paper. Next week is Israel's thirty-ninth Independence Day, and a flag on a nearby streetlight already waves and cracks in the wind. The two stand facing me, small, thin, and drowsy. Their exhaustion makes them look even more juvenile. The last of the partyers are returning from the Tel Aviv nightclubs to their homes in Herzlia, Netanya, and Haifa. Israel sleeps. On the nearby Tel Baruch road, cars honk at the prostitutes. When I ask them about the prostitutes, they are very confused. Better to jerk off, they explain seriously, than to get syphilis or that new thing.

"All this is yours for now?" I ask, indicating the building. They boast: "We are responsible for everything here. We can turn on all the televisions and the VCRs. We can eat anything in the kitchen, make telephone calls to anywhere, but we don't know anyone we can call."

That, too, is one of the absurd parts of the situation: wherever they go, people are suspicious of these Arab workers, and search them, restrict their movement, and make their lives miserable, but on the other hand, there are long hours every day, all night, in which they get the keys to everything from us.

"How often do you see your parents?"

"We go home once a month. For the weekend. We visit family, friends. Sleep at night.

"My friends go to school. I couldn't go to school, because things are hard at home. I bring all the money I earn to my father. I put a little aside for myself that he doesn't know about. I miss my mother most of all. My mother is worth the whole world."

I ask them if they know what the place they work in is. It's like a school, they say, a sort of university or college. Have they ever seen the students who study here? No. We always leave before they come. I light them cigarettes through the fence, and they return to the large building, Samir taller and 'Ali slightly bent over behind him, dragging their feet inch by inch up the stairs. Like a boy with a teddy bear trudging his way to bed.

16

The Terrorist's

Father

Mohammed Ali Al-Kal'ilah is a man of forty-nine, tall and of noble bearing. He was born in the village of Samu'a, twenty kilometers south of Hebron. The village has a population of ten thousand, all of them Moslems who earn their livelihoods from farming and from the large stone quarries next to the village. They send the cut stones to Jordan, and someone once said that this, too, is a way of returning the territories to that country.

The security forces arrested Mohammed Ali Al-Kal'ilah in June 1985. He worked as a room attendant in a Dead Sea hotel and was taken from there to a prison in Hebron and placed in a cell. He told me his story in Hebrew.

"A few guys came to me, as if they wanted to beat me up, and said, You are a dog and a son of a dog, and I said, What for? They said, You don't know why we brought you here? Where is your son? I said, My son was home with me about three weeks ago, and afterwards, he went back to his house in Ramallah. He has a house there where he lives with his wife and children. They said, No, no. Tell us where he is now."

The son, Ali Mohammed Al-Shehade Al-Kal'ilah, left his father's house in Samu'a when he was eighteen years old and rented a house in Ramallah. He lived there with his wife—who was a teacher—and with his three children—'Afaf, Mohammed, and 'Amar.

"They said, We want your son, and only you know where he is. I said, I don't know. They said, You are a whore and a son of a whore and a dog. They came to beat me, and someone said, 'Don't beat him, he'll tell everything soon. I said, I don't know anything. They said, We'll bring your wife here and we'll fuck her in front of you. This went on for almost a week, only talk, without beatings at all.

"After that, they said suddenly, Now go, bring your wife, and your son's wife, and sit here, in the office of the *mukhabarat*, the intelligence service, in Hebron, every day from seven in the morning to seven in the evening. So I brought them, and there was also my son's baby, and officers pass us the whole time and spit on us and say, Tfu! you are dogs and the sons of dogs, and every day they would leave us there until nine at night, and every day we had to take a taxi, and when we came home at night, the *mukhabarat* would come again, at four in the morning, and enter the house, and pull everything out of the closets, wake up the children, and they would bring big dogs with them and say, We want your children to see the dogs and go crazy from fear of them.

"After that, the daily detention in Hebron ended, but the *mukhabarat* would still come to search the house every night. And after about three months I went again to the hotel at the Dead Sea to work, and I heard on television that the army had a battle with some people near Hebron, killed four and captured one wounded, and my wife called me on the telephone and said to come back, and I went and I saw my house bulldozed, not one stone left on another."

Why were they searching for your son? What had he done?

"They say he killed Israelis. I don't know. He never said anything."

You really don't know? Even now you don't know?

"I don't know! I didn't even get along with him. He never spoke to me."

This is the story: The son, Ali, was arrested in April 1978, accused of membership in the Fatah, and released. He claimed that he had been freed on the basis of a certain bargain, and he apparently did not live up to it. He was arrested again in 1979, accused of the original crime, and sentenced to four months in prison, with another half year suspended.

From the moment he was released, he was a marked man: on the one hand, the security forces watched his every step, and on the other hand, his former friends tormented him, accusing him of collaborating with the enemy. No one spoke to him. He was a pariah. A person who met him during that time testified that he seemed as if he had gone mad. He lived like a hunted beast, and sensed that every passing moment brought his end that much closer. It may be that for some the occupation, with its cruel demands, is a challenge which hardens their souls and pride; but there are, without a doubt, many more who, caught between the conqueror and the conquered, lose their humanity.

In order to counter the accusations of his friends, the young man went out to the mountains and made contact with a particularly deadly gang of terrorists, a gang which a year previously had murdered a Jew in Ramallah.

Ali Al-Shehade Al-Kal'ilah took part in the gang's horrifying murders of two couples, one in a forest near the town of Beit Shemesh (within the 1967 boundaries of Israel), and another not far away, near the settlement of Mavo Beitar, in the West Bank.

When I learned, a week after my conversation with the father, what his son had actually done, I felt that I didn't want to hear the rest of the story from the father. I remembered the innocent, naive, and optimistic faces of the murdered couples, and I could not find in myself any sympathy at all for Ali Al-Kal'ilah's father, lamenting his son and demanding that he be allowed to rebuild his destroyed house.

I refused to even think about him for three weeks. The deed was like an open, coagulating wound. I thought: So they knocked down his house, big deal! I reserve my sympathy for the real victims, for his son's victims. I refused to go back to see him.

But after three weeks, during which I met so many Arabs and Jews, dogmatically miserable and some unaware of how miserable they are, I sank deeper and deeper into frustration and melancholy, and the futility of the unbreakable prison of circumstance, without a solution and without an outlet, only continual pain, an ongoing and spreading terror. I then understood that I had to go back to Mohammed Ali Al-Kal'ilah; to go back to him precisely because of the repulsion and repugnance I felt, and hear his story to the end, because it is a story that repeats itself in a thousand and one variations, the hard and evil story in which there are no victors, and in which no one is in the right, only death and destruction and people who are bound to their fate with a curse.

Mohammed Ali Al-Kal'ilah is a tall, mustached man, a man with presence. Swollen, purple bags under his eyes. He had a four-room house and a large garden in Samu'a. In the garden he grew figs, grapes, olives, and vegetables. The rooms were carpeted with rugs his wife wove with her own hands. It took her four months to make each rug.

One morning, soldiers came to the house and notified her that she had fifteen minutes to get all her belongings and her daughters out of the house, after which the house would be leveled. Sometimes, when I hear about the destruction of houses in the West Bank, I wonder what I would remove from my house during that quarter hour— the basic necessities, I suppose: bed linens and cooking utensils. But what about the photograph albums? And my manuscript? And books? And old letters? How much can you get out in a frenzied fifteen minutes?

Al-Kal'ilah's wife took mattresses and blankets, plates and a gas burner, and a suitcase full of clothes into which she had the presence of mind to shove the family photo album. She and her two daughters, Ibtasam and Noel, stood there and cried. The soldiers knocked down the house and spread its stones over the entire garden. The head of the family arrived after the destruction. A neighbor offered the family accommodations in a single room in his house. As Mohammed Al-Kal'ilah stood by the ruins of his house, security personnel approached him once more. "They told me, Come, you son-of-a-bitch, come with us now. I said, What more do you want from me? He said, We killed your son. I said, Fine, you're strong, you can kill us all. I'm only one man and you are a government. They handcuffed me and took me for interrogation in Hebron. I said, I don't have anything to tell you, I haven't seen my son for a long time. They showed me my son's identity card covered with blood, and said, Look, this is his blood. Now tell us where he was during the months when we didn't know where he was.

"I said, I don't know. They don't believe me. And I was like a dead man, because my son had been killed, my house had been destroyed, and at work they told me not to come back. What do I have left, what?

"They interrogated me. Beat me with their hands all over my body and threw me hard against the wall. Afterwards, I would sit in a chair—and they would come suddenly from behind and throw me over. The interrogator would sit across from me in a high chair. He would present the sole of his army boot to me, and then press down on my balls hard and harder, and spit on me from above, from head to foot, and when he had no more spit he would go drink a cup of coffee and come back and spit some more.

"Later, they put me on trial and gave me four months in jail, because they said I helped my son hide in my house, but I didn't help him, he didn't hide in my house, because he had his own house in Ramallah, and even the *mukhabarat* knew he had not been with me for years, and even if he murdered all the Israelis, he is the only one responsible for what he did. Why did they knock down my house? Why did they destroy my body in the interrogations after he died? Who does it help that they kill me, too? Why do they have to do that?"

In the Emergency Defense Regulations of 1945 (promulgated by the King in his Privy Council), part 12, section 119, it says: "A military commander may issue an order confiscating for the government of Israel any house, building, or land, if there is reason to believe that any firearm was illegally fired from it, or from which were illegally thrown, detonated, exploded, or shot in any other way a bomb, hand grenade, or any other explosive or inflammable device, or any house, building, or land situated in any area, city, village, neighborhood, or street, in which it has been discovered that the inhabitants, or some of them, violated, or tried to violate, or assisted violators, or were accomplices after the fact to the violation of these regulations, violations involving violence or threats of violence or any violation judged in a military court; with the confiscation of the house or building or land as stated above, the commander may destroy the house or building or anything within the house . . ."

The wording of the regulations allows, in fact, the destruction of any structure in any village or city in which one resident has committed any security violation; the commander may order that the house be destroyed, confiscated, or sealed without having to give any notification, and without charging the owner of the house with any crime.

"Now they won't allow me to build myself a new house. They say, Someone like you can't get a permit. We now live in a rented house, two rooms without a kitchen and without a bathroom. Eight people together with my wife and my son's children, and we cook everything in the bedroom. They made us into animals. Now tell me what law you have that doesn't let a man build a house for himself? And not only that—you killed a man, why don't you give him to his parents? Why don't you tell them where he is buried? What more do you want? Are you afraid of his body? Let us know at least that he has a grave. Even if he is a murderer, he is still our son."

Attorney Leah Tsemel, who has taken on Al-Kal'ilah's case, has submitted uncountable petitions to the authorities, and asked why his house was destroyed. On January 12, 1987, the laconic answer arrived: "The petitioner's son resided in the destroyed house." In March of this year, Tsemel appealed to the High Court of Justice. The hearing on the petition has not yet taken place.

I have told the story as it was told to me. One's heart does not go out to Mohammed Al-Kal'ilah, who raised such a son. But perhaps one must take a rational, principled stand here precisely because he arouses no sympathy. It is a difficult thing to do, nerve-racking to the hearer of the story. To the entire Israeli ethos. It is precisely the exceptional, repugnant cases like these which are the real forge of a moral and human code of behavior. To display wide-hearted humanism even in such cases, and reduce somewhat the hate and bitterness.

I did not, however, tell this story for any purpose. If I had a goal in mind, I could have chosen a much less ambiguous incident. There is no lack of them. I chose this story because it is a sort of bitter microcosm of the big story—of two nations' life together. One that brings to life the simple misery in which we live.

Attorney Leah Tsemel is still trying to get the terrorist's body. "I have a few bodies like that I haven't gotten yet," she says, as a sort of grotesque conclusion to the whole story. There is a cemetery near Jericho for terrorists, and for prisoners who died in hunger strikes from improper forced feedings. Mohammed Ali Al-Kal'ilah goes every day to see the ruins of his house. I cannot even begin to measure the sorrow of the families of the murdered. I know that a family which has lost a dear one in such a way has no life. I think of the young, full lives which were cut off. I do not know if the families of the victims find any comfort in fostering hatred of the murderer, his family, his nation. How can we judge them if that is how they feel? The murderer's father said to me: "If my son murdered, kill him. Kill him immediately! But why have you destroyed my entire life? Why have you made me and my family into beasts? I still have power in my hands"—he clenched his fist for me and trembled—"I could kill a million times the man who ordered my house destroyed. Did I ever do anything like that? Did I ever think like that before? I only wanted to live. Now they have made me like that, too. They have turned me into a murderer."

I asked him how he supports his family now, after he was fired. At first, he did not want to answer. Afterwards, he said he had become a beggar. He goes from village to village and pleads for money. Not in Samu'a. He is ashamed to go there. Sometimes he goes to a village and sits in the street, and someone he knows passes. Both of them turn their heads in shame.

17

Last Night There
Was an Inferno Here

The West Bank was a storm during the entire month before the attack at Alfei Menashe. There were daily demonstrations and arrests, stone throwings and tire burnings. Three thousand security prisoners were in the midst of a hunger strike in the military jails. The entire population was restive over the strike. Disaster was in the air, inescapable; whoever traveled the West Bank roads at that time felt it. One Friday, as I exited the village of Dura, an explosive device went off there; a week later, as I returned from Kfar Adumim, stones were thrown at my car. On our way to Nablus, the Israeli cabdriver took a large, black-and-white checked kaffi-yeh, the traditional Arab headdress, out of his glove compartment and spread it conspicuously over his dashboard. To fool the enemy, he said, so that they stop to think before they start throwing stones.

The disaster occurred on the Saturday night before Passover. The Moses family was traveling in its car from the settlement Alfei Menashe to neighboring Kfar Saba. As they left the settlement, a Molotov cocktail was thrown at the car, apparently from an orange grove along the road. The car burst into flames. The father, his clothes on fire, succeeded in getting his children out of the car. The mother, Ofra, thirty-five years old, five months pregnant, was trapped and perished. The survivors are still suffering from serious burns: the father, sons Adi and Nir, and the son of friends, Yosef Hillel. Five-year-old Tal died in July.

The morning after the attack, three military cars are parked alongside the road to the settlement. Senior officers survey the area through dark sunglasses. They converse in post-disaster low voices. On the road, an ugly black stain, composed of the remains of a burnt tire and a timid wreath of three flowers in the middle of the spot.

The businesslike presence of serious-faced security men fills the area. Roadblocks, searches, the crackle of walkie-talkies, a patrol plane flying above. A curfew has been declared in the nearby Arab city of Qalqilia, and in the surrounding villages. Two gray army bulldozers knock down the first rows of trees in the orange groves on both sides of the road. In one of them, apparently, the thrower of the Molotov cocktail lay in wait. As of this writing, he has yet to be caught.

It is possible, on the basis of past experience, to sketch his portrait. It is possible to re-create the words those who sent him poured into his heart in order to seal it, so that it might serve as a deadly, blind instrument. In his friends' eyes, he will from this point on be a hero. A freedom fighter. The situation is a mint casting human coins with opposite legends imprinted on their two sides. But the contradicting legends do not change the fact that between them—freedom fighter or terrorist; ours or theirs—can be found the dark, hidden raw material: a murderer.

This morning the air is perfumed by the flowering orange groves, and the land's breath awakens the abundance of springtime and the exorbitant profusion of nature. The pale roots of the orange trees break through the wounded ground, and green oranges still roll earthward, coming to rest on a carpet of wildflowers.

Four hundred and fifty families live in Alfei Menashe. Three and a half years ago they came to the bald, boulder-crowned mountain. Rows of houses are stuck in a semicircle on the side of the hill, and from far off, in the glare of the sun, they look like the sparkling hooks of a net thrown over the neck of a huge gray whale.

Close up, one sees that the whale has surrendered: roads and public parks, playgrounds, houses surrounded by green, a shopping center for morning chats and cultural evenings, and in the schoolyard boys play soccer.

The settlement Alfei Menashe is located very close to Kfar Saba and looks much like one of the neighborhoods of private houses which surround, for instance, Jerusalem. "We are, after all, included in the Alon Plan," say the residents, surprised, referring to the compromise borders proposed by then Foreign Minister Yigael Alon in 1976, under which Israel would absorb parts of the West Bank. "We aren't settlers at all!" As if they don't understand how the terrorists could mistake them for such—how did they not understand that they are included within the consensus?

The residents of Alfei Menashe do reside, as they say, within the area about which there is general agreement. They are like tens of thousands of other Israelis who now live over the Green Line for reasons of convenience and quality of life, rather than as a matter of ideology. Another practical nibble at the moral problem, another step toward surrounding the immoral with the amoral. In ten more years, if the present situation continues, it will become clear that the motherly, broad down blanket of the consensus is actually made of rubber, and there will always be those who will not stop stretching it more and more, from five minutes from Kfar Saba to a stone's throw from Sidon.

At night there was an inferno here. After the attack the residents of Alfei Menashe and of other settlements gathered to take revenge. First they cut down two trees in the nearby orange grove, "to symbolize the cutting down of an Israeli family," and afterwards, while the smoking car still lay on the road, they entered the nearby Arab city of Qalqilia. In their words, they "burned four piles of weeds." The press reported burning fields and broken windows in hundreds of cars and homes, and the frightening of the inhabitants of Qalqilia and a nearby village, Hablah.

Shaul Hai from Alfei Menashe took part in those actions. "What happened? What's the big deal? Did we kill anyone? Did we take an eye for an eye? Did we even slap an Arab in the face? If you were to go to Qalqilia today, you would see the truth. I'm a moderate type, I swear, but when I see something like that—a whole family . . ." He fell silent, biting his lip. "I ask the bleeding hearts, those who are now shouting that we took the law into our own hands, what have they done to prevent this situation? What have you done, what?"

And what happened in Qalqilia? And what did you do in Hablah?

"Settlers from Karnei Shomron and Kdumim went there. The army—which always fights us instead of the terrorists—stopped their cars, so they got out and went on by foot, over the fields. They only went into the city and into Hablah and burned piles of weeds, and afterwards I read in the newspaper about burning fields in Qalqilia! What would they do to those Arabs in a case like that in Russia? Bang bang bang bang bang! To the wall, no questions asked! No one would open his mouth! I'm telling you—good for those guys who gave it to the Arabs—they really know how to put things straight. You can't put out a fire with polite talk!" He leaves me, boiling with anger, and I don't know which fire he was talking about: The car? The desire for revenge? The large barrel of gunpowder?

I try to imagine those moments last night, in Kdumim: the telephone in the settlement's office rings. "There has been an attack. One or more dead. Not clear how many. Have to notify. Have to do something." The whisper turns into a rumble. People run quickly, grimly, from house to house. The air thickens as everyone becomes part of a taut web of nerves. The news passes silently from person to person. From settlement to settlement. The men get in their cars (which immediately become "transports"). At the gate, someone ducks his head into the car and says in a hushed voice that he just now talked with a leading figure in Gush Emunim and he will be there, too. That grants an unspoken official seal of approval. I imagine that they did not talk much in the car about what was about to happen. The people already know that there will be an investigation, because that's how the authorities work, that no one here will actually give the order. So that no one person will be culpable.

In this way a sort of collective, agreed-upon distance from the decision is created. They allow the violence to pulsate in its raw form, shapeless, in the fear and the hope that it will work itself, direct the hands and blind the eyes and hearts, and force them to act in one pre-determined way.

Do I not already know all the heroes of this tragedy? The murderous terrorist, whose brothers in hatred I have met so many times in Nablus, in Hebron, in Deheisha; and those who set out for revenge, to correct a crime with an injustice, the determined, history-conscious peo-ple from Ofra, from Kfar Adumim; and the poor family itself, the children, the parents, and the innocent inhab-itants of Qalqilia, taking cover in their houses in fright, listening to the approaching footsteps?

I knew them all, and I could speak with all of them, as well as find similarities and sympathy between us. But now every eye is bloodshot, they are all possessed, the slaves of a single power, tyrannical and cruel, leading them, blinded, one into the other.

I enter Qalqilia. It is my first time in a city under curfew. It is strange to pace through complete stillness, when every step sounds as if it breaks the surface of a frozen puddle. Everything is locked up—the stores and the houses. Human footsteps no longer sound in the street. And spring bursts into this emptiness with all its might, flowing like a drunken crowd through the empty streets and alleys, its butterflies, the colors and perfumes of its flowers, and for a moment it is possible to err and wonder whether the city has only been drugged by the abundant, sensuous perfume, addicted to it, dizzy and loose-limbed like Jericho.

A pretty city, Qalqilia, fair to the eye. Well kept. Roses flower in enclosures along the main boulevard. There are no signs of violence. I do not see broken windows or the remains of a fire, even though the settlers themselves said they came here as a great and angry group.

Suddenly a boy leaps from the doorway of a house in a narrow alley and runs to the road. Hey, boy, don't you know there's a curfew? Yes, yes, I know, but I slept at night at my aunt's house, and I want to go home, and not only that, I'm not a boy, I'm a girl!

You're a girl?

"Yes!"

She is truly insulted.

Fine, fine. Excuse me that I didn't notice. But your hair is very short.

"Yes, but I'm wearing earrings!"

And she presents the tiny earrings, sparkling in her earlobes, for my inspection. No doubt about it—a girl.

I apologize once more. Her name is Samah, and she is nine years old. She is not afraid to run, because the army isn't in this side street, and not only that, they won't do anything to her, because she is little.

Do you know what happened here at night?

Her fresh, mischievous face locks. Don't know. Didn't hear anything.

Were you afraid?

Yes, but only because her aunt cried all night. Now she has to run.

I follow her with my eyes as she crosses the street. She looks both ways, and afterwards, speedily, like a trained fighter, like a hare crossing an open field, she rushes, slightly bowed, and disappears. What life teaches.

Now I begin making out heads peeking from roofs,

from the balcony railings, from the half-closed blinds. The alley next to the Shalom Café is closed at present, and I exchange a few words with a family hiding behind a slightly open iron gate. They did not hear anything; at night there were cries and shots and they smelled smoke. The Jews' cars sped past, honking. Then the army came, and the inhabitants calmed down, because the army is less dangerous than the *mustawtanin*, the settlers; soldiers passed and announced over loudspeakers that there would be a curfew. Until when? Don't know. Maybe one day, maybe two. Until further notice. They did not sleep all night out of fear. There is also a problem—Grandmother is in bed upstairs and she has pains in her chest, maybe it's her heart, she is crying from the pain, and they cannot bring a doctor.

I ask if they know what happened yesterday on the road by Alfei Menashe. No. They don't know. They only heard that the Jews tore things apart. "Someone burned a family with small children on the road. They killed a woman," I say. Once again I find myself facing an expression emptying itself of all emotion, like a door slammed in my face. "We don't know anything. We haven't heard anything."

On the main street, I am surprised to see televisions, refrigerators, and ovens on the sidewalk, outside a closed store. Across the street, furniture: armchairs, beds, and mattresses. Two soldiers call me over and ask who I am. In those places where the storekeepers did not manage to get their merchandise into the store before having to lock up, the army has stationed guards to prevent plundering. This mixture of violence and consideration, of brutality and basic humanity is what makes everything hard to deal with and hard to understand. It is even harder for those who do the work themselves. Is this an army of occupation, or a police force protecting citizens from their own fellow nationals? What does a young soldier (maybe a farmer's son) feel when he has to cut down young trees? What does an Arab feel as he labors on the construction site of a new settlement on the hill overlooking his village? What kind of occupying army can it be whose soldiers did not rape a single woman from among its surrendering enemies? What does the student reservist, who studies together with Arabs at the Hebrew University, feel when he suddenly has to shoot into a crown of demonstrators at An-Najah University in Nablus?

Another question: Into what reality are children to be educated? How fuzzy can the lesson I give to my sons be? Maybe I do them an injustice when I bring them up with certain values and do not prepare them for the brutal life we live here?

And a last question: Is the feeling that the situation cannot possibly continue forever really a reasonable guarantee that it will eventually change?

The secretariat of Gush Emunim and the heads of the Jewish settlements in the West Bank and Gaza Strip meet in the gymnasium of the school in Alfei Menashe. They are all here, those whose names you see in the newspapers, and many of their friends. They damn the army, the Chief of Staff, the Minister of Defense, and the entire government with fire and brimstone. They sit around tables in the gym, between ladders and vaulting horses, their faces red with fury, fingering their pistols. They know that at such moments it is easy for an unsure government, overwhelmed with guilt, to give in to their demands, and they strike the iron while it's hot. You can understand their motives, but they are repellent. Most of the residents of Alfei Menashe that I spoke to wanted nothing to do with this political convention, exploiting their sorrow for its own purposes—most of them boycotted it.

Hooliganism echoes in everything the leaders of Gush Emunim say. A smooth, sharp hooliganism, but hooliganism nonetheless. With television cameras in the gymnasium, every speaker makes sure to give lip service to "the need to work within the law," but they pronounce the words like someone spitting a rotten piece of apple from his mouth.

Rav Levinger, leader of the Jewish settlement in Hebron, his beard stiff and wiry, his face red, calls the Minister of Defense a murderer. His hands spilled this blood. Levinger hints that another Jewish underground will arise. It will arise because of the government's failures. "They decided that there would not be another underground, and I accepted the decision," he declares and hints. He accepted but did not agree. "But today we once again face a situation in which the Ministry of Defense has made us fair game, and the Ministry of Defense bears, after all, the major share of the guilt for the last underground." Those were his words. Maybe one of the young people of Gush Emunim understood the hint the Rav dangled before them, and afterwards the people of Gush Emunim will be shocked and say that their entire system of education opposes violence.

"If we allow ourselves to get used to stone throwing," Levinger seethed, "we will get used to funerals. One funeral and another and another. Blood and more blood and more blood!" His finger jabs the air as if he were debating a passage of Talmud. His head bobs constantly, as if drawing something out of the depths of his being, as if he has drilled through his soul to its primal layer, even deeper and wilder, where lies all the sediment of Jewish suffering and an incomparably dark thirst for revenge. And now he straightens his neck and sputters death. We need a death penalty! Death penalty! Why are you afraid of the death penalty? In the United States they execute lots of people!"

Beside the preacher of death, Daniella Weiss, Secretary-General of Gush Emunim, nods and her eyes sparkle, two rings of red raised on her cheeks, but it seems to me it is not the spring that is bringing out this bloom. She repeats his words, her eyes hanging on his lips, her lips moving, as if she is the only one who knows how to read his words, death penalty! It is a short distance from seeing these two move opposite each other in the stylized movements of a sacrificial revenge ceremony.

Elyakim Ha-etzni, a Kiryat Arba leader, stands and froths before the assembly, but his voice is so high that the echoes bouncing off the walls of the gymnasium crash into each other and it is very hard to hear what he is saying. It is almost certainly fascinating—it seems that he has prepared a list of steps the authorities must take against PLO activists in the territories, and maybe against anyone who has ambitions which clash with Ha-etzni's. I make out the words "expulsion," "closure," "imprisonment," "death penalty," "destruction," and for a short, mad moment I see Ha-etzni prancing happily through a West Bank completely emptied of people.

Someone else rises to speak. A resident of Alfei Menashe, a lieutenant colonel in the standing army, large-bodied and with a sympathetic face, the face of a golden boy of the land of Israel, and as his speech takes off, his face becomes more serious and harsh, and he concludes by promising that he himself, and all residents of the settlement, will deal with the Arab villages in the area "with all the means at our disposal." "We will go in there like commandos!" he roars, his finger waving in the air. The journalists take it all down.

Then the funeral. Alfei Menashe still does not have a cemetery, so Ofra was buried in Segula. Two soldiers who fell in the Lebanese War are also buried there. Somber and bitter. The crowd treads silently. The husband and the children are still fighting for their lives in the hospital. Meir Kahane arrives. He frequents burials. He strides, surrounded by a few strange, tense young men, both drawing and repelling everyone's glances, like an embarrassing subconscious failing.

We pace along the cemetery paths, and Haim Korfu, Minister of Transportation and the government's flesh-and-blood representative, drives among us in his Volvo. To my left I hear Ha-etzni explaining to someone how Israeli peace initiatives of the past and present have only caused more Jewish deaths: "When I heard Peres's idea of an international peace conference, I immediately knew there would be more victims." I peer at him, and try to figure out where he plugs in the device that allows him to make such logical contortions—and wonder whether the misfunction is mine.

The government's representative speaks by the grave: "Just as the two soldiers who fell yesterday died in defense of the safety of the Galilee, you, Ofra, fell in defense of the safety of Jerusalem."

I find it hard to believe my ears: "You, Ofra, are our

soldier . . . We established settlements in order to make
Judea and Samaria safer . . ." These words seem so
foreign to the pain, and to the facts. "The settlements
are a guarantee against the Palestinian state of those
who hate us!" Korfu declares, and someone shouts at
him: "You are Peres's whores, all of you!" He is silenced
by those who stand around him. Relatives sob. They
almost certainly do not take in Korfu's words. Like standard words of greeting and curses. I hope they do not
hear it. What can they feel when their dead loved one
turns into the instrument of a cynical political game?
Why does there have to be a government representative
at such a tragic event? Is death also the government's
domain? Do the living also partake in this same hollow
protocol? Why do politicians not know how to make
themselves scarce, and shamefacedly withdraw from the
place of the pain and sorrow which they, in their im-
potence, have a part in causing?

I listen to the government representative and begin to
understand. There is no guarantee that what has to be
done here to prevent more and more suffering will actually be done. Most of the tragedies which have befallen
nations happened because of the mistakes those peoples
made. There is a no-man's-land, a dead place, dividing
personal pain, a man and his feelings, from the place in
which things are decided and the agreements and party
manifestos and official eulogies are drafted. "The PLO
wants to cut us off at the roots, but we will do the same
to them!" Korfu concludes the official prayer of the government representative at the cemetery.

The funeral has ended, it was announced. Then there
was total stillness. The crowd waited as if for some sign,
for an event that would carry off all its emotions in a

storm. Violence waited above like a torch sputtering in the wind. The air was filled for a moment with the flatulent whisper "Kahane." Then the tension subsided. The crowd began to disperse. Korfu sailed off in his car, and the television crew folded up its equipment.

The sun was covered by a slight cloud, shimmering through it, as if covered by a handkerchief. Ofra Moses's close friends and relatives quietly approached the grave. Now they were alone, without politicians and functionaries and merchants of tragedy. The close friends gathered into a tight group, embracing and solid in their pain around the small, long mound of earth, and tightened their circle more and more, gazing inconsolable and unbelieving at the new scar on the ground.

18

The First

Twenty Years

I belong to the generation that celebrated its bar mitz-vah during the Six-Day War. Then, in 1967, the surging energy of our adolescent hormones was coupled with the intoxication gripping the entire country; the con-quest, the confident penetration of the enemy's land, his complete surrender, breaking the taboo of the border, imperiously striding through the narrow streets of cities until now forbidden, and the smells, the primal view, and that same erotic tingle latent in every first meeting between conqueror and conquered—ah, what a sen-suous explosion of all the pent-up desire that was in us! And on a grand scale! With the entire country!

We were thirteen years old, and we reached maturity in a collective rite of passage together with the adults. Secret desires and fears broke out into the sunlight and became sensible. Only a month before, in May, we had watched a military parade of the Israeli Defense Forces in the streets of Jerusalem: because of the cease-fire agreement with Jordan, armor and aircraft could not be brought into the city, and so the representatives of those forces had to be satisfied with displaying cardboard cut-outs of planes and tanks. What poor proxies they were!

Afterwards, everything happened.

And in twenty years, everything happens, and it is as if nothing happens at all.

Seven years ago, I felt I had to write something about the occupation. I could not understand how an entire nation like mine, an enlightened nation by all accounts, is able to train itself to live as a conqueror without making its own life wretched. What happened to us? How were they able to pass their values on to me during these years? For two years I sat and worked out those thoughts and dilemmas of mine. I wrote a novel, *The Smile of the Lamb*, and the more I wrote, the more I understood that the occupation is a continuing and stubborn test for both sides trapped in it. It is the sphinx lying at the entrance to each of us, demanding that we give a clear answer. That we take a stand and make a decision. Or at least relate. The book was a sort of answer to the riddle of my sphinx.

Years passed, and I discovered that one does not have to battle that sphinx. That you can go mad if you allow it to torture you with questions day and night. And there were other matters, and other things to write about and do. Because there are other sphinxes as well.

So I also became an artist of sublimation. I found myself developing the same voluntary suspension of questions about ethics and occupation. I did not visit the territories; I did not even go to Old Jerusalem. Because I felt the hatred of the people there, but mostly because I cannot tolerate relations that are not on an equal basis. Like so many others, I began to think of that kidney-shaped expanse of land, the West Bank, as an organ transplanted into my body against my wishes, and about which soon, when I had time, I would come to some sort of conclusion and decision. Of course, that transplanted organ continued to produce antibodies in my consciousness. I also knew how to declaim the familiar words meant to satisfy old sphinxes: it cannot go on this way, the occupation corrupts us, we have created a system of masters and slaves, and so on. But the furnace which forged those words went out and cooled long ago, and I did not want to feel it.

I took on this seven-week journey through the West Bank at the suggestion of *Koteret Rashit*, an Israeli newsweekly, because I understand that my sphinx had become a spayed cat purring contentedly at my feet. Because the worn sentences that I used like so many other people, though true, seemed now to be something else: like the walls of a penitentiary that I built around a reality I do not want to know; like jailers I stationed in order to protect myself from a gray world now repugnant to me. Suddenly I discovered that some jailers and criminals create—after years of living together and becoming accustomed to each other—unholy alliances. But I am in great danger from this, too, so I wanted to go to the places which most haunted me. Into the heart of the harsh clash between Jew and Arab. To see things with my own eyes in order to write about them. At first I thought they were not so terrible. Maybe only a mountain shadow which seems to us to be a mountain. If so, it must be told. And if not, even more so. After sharing my experience, the reader may decide to stand by his previous opinions, but he will have to take note of the price he pays, and what he has until now been prepared to ignore.

In another thirteen years there will be two million Arabs under Israeli rule in the West Bank and Gaza Strip. In 2010 their number will equal ours.

There are those who say it is possible to continue on in this way for years. That over the years the "fabric of life" (mutual acquaintance, economic links, and so on) will overcome enmity. That is idiocy, and reality proves it even now. As long as the present "fabric of life" continues, it is wrapped around an iron fist of hate and revenge.

The argument based on the "fabric of life," which now seems sober, pragmatic, almost businesslike, is a very dangerous argument for us, the Israelis. It turns the matter of the territories from an immoral matter into an amoral matter. It corrupts and anesthetizes us. One day we will wake up to a bitter surprise.

I want to go off on a tangent and tell a little story about this "fabric of life."

An Arab woman cleans the stairwell at the housing project in which I live. Her name is Amuna, and she lives in Ramallah. I talk to her from time to time. A three-year-old boy, the son of one of the neighbors, used to seeing her bent over a pail of water, heard us talking and was surprised—I saw it on his face. He asked her name and I told him. Afterwards, he asked what we had talked about in Arabic, and I explained. He thought a minute and said: "Amuna is a little bit a person and a little bit a dog, right?" I asked him why he said that. He explained: "She is a little bit a dog, because she always walks on all fours. And she is also a little bit a person, because she knows how to talk."

End of story.

So what will be?

I can only guess, and be aided by what I know—not about the situation, but about people.

I have a bad feeling: I am afraid that the current situation will continue exactly as it is for another ten or twenty years. There is one excellent guarantee of that— human idiocy and the desire not to see the approaching danger. But I am also sure that the moment will come when we will be forced to do something, and it may well be that our position then will be much less favorable than it is now.

It is not a question of who is right, we or they, right or left. It is a question of facts and numbers, and a few other things beyond facts and numbers, things in the fuzzy area between dogs and people. Whoever does not agree to speculate in this way about the future need only glance backward. The history of the world proves that the situation we preserve here cannot last for long. And if it lasts, it will exact a deadly price.

When I left on this journey, I decided not to talk with Jewish or Arab politicians or officials. Their positions are well known to the point of weariness. I wanted to meet the people who are themselves the real players in the drama, those who pay first the price of their actions and failures, courage, cowardliness, corruption, nobility. I quickly understood that we all pay the price, but not all of us know it.

We have lived for twenty years in a false and artificial situation, based on illusions, on a teetering center of gravity between hate and fear, in a desert void of emotion and consciousness, and the passing time turns slowly into a separate, forbidding entity hanging above us like a suffocating layer of yellow dust. From this point of view, nothing matches the occupation as a great personal challenge. As a personal crossroads demanding action and thought. Sometimes you can gain in this way—for a split second—real mountain air.

Albert Camus said that this passage from speech to moral action has a name. "To become human." During the last weeks, and seeing what I saw, I wondered more than once how many times during the last twenty years I had been worthy of being called human, and how many people among the millions participating in this drama are worthy of it.